OUR WORLD IN PICTURES

THE HISTORY BOOK

DK SMITHSONIAN ✺

OUR WORLD IN PICTURES

THE HISTORY BOOK

WRITTEN BY **SUFIYA AHMED, PETER CHRISP,
JENNY COX, SEUN MATILUKO, ANDREA MILLS**

DK DELHI
Senior Editors Virien Chopra, Neha Ruth Samuel
Senior Art Editor Shreya Anand
Project Art Editor Sanjay Chauhan
Art Editors Revati Anand, Sanya Jain
Assistant Editor Arpit Aggarwal
Project Picture Researcher Nishwan Rasool
Picture Researcher Geetika Bhandari
Picture Research Manager Taiyaba Khatoon
Managing Editor Kingshuk Ghoshal
Managing Art Editor Govind Mittal
DTP Coordinator Shanker Prasad
DTP Designers Nand Kishore Acharya, Rakesh Kumar
Pre-production Manager Balwant Singh
Production Manager Pankaj Sharma
Jacket Designer Tanya Mehrotra
Senior Jackets Coordinator Priyanka Sharma Saddi
Editorial Head Glenda Fernandes
Design Head Malavika Talukder

DK LONDON
Senior Editor Sam Atkinson
Senior Art Editor Jacqui Swan
Senior US Editor Megan Douglass
US Executive Editor Lori Cates Hand
Picture Researchers Nic Dean, Sarah Hopper
Managing Editor Rachel Fox
Managing Art Editor Owen Peyton Jones
Senior Production Editor Andy Hilliard
Senior Production Controller Meskerem Berhane
Jacket Design Development Manager Sophia MTT
Publisher Andrew Macintyre
Associate Publishing Director Liz Wheeler
Art Director Karen Self
Publishing Director Jonathan Metcalf

Authors Sufiya Ahmed, Peter Chrisp,
Jenny Cox, Seun Matiluko, Andrea Mills
Consultant Philip Parker

First American Edition, 2023
Published in the United States by DK Publishing
1745 Broadway, 20th Floor, New York, NY 10019

Copyright © 2023 Dorling Kindersley Limited
DK, a Division of Penguin Random House LLC
23 24 25 26 27 10 9 8 7 6 5 4 3 2 1
001-334049-May/2023

A catalog record for this book is available from the Library of Congress.
ISBN 978-0-7440-7631-8

DK books are available at special discounts when purchased in bulk
for sales promotions, premiums, fund-raising, or educational use.
For details, contact: DK Publishing Special Markets,
1745 Broadway, 20th Floor, New York, NY 10019
SpecialSales@dk.com

Printed and bound in Malaysia

For the curious
www.dk.com

Smithsonian

Established in 1846, the Smithsonian is
the world's largest museum and research
complex, dedicated to public education, national
service, and scholarship in the arts, sciences,
and history. It includes 21 museums and
galleries and the National Zoological Park.
The total number of artifacts, works of art, and
specimens in the Smithsonian's collection is
estimated at 155.5 million.

MIX
Paper | Supporting
responsible forestry
FSC™ C018179

This book was made with Forest
Stewardship Council™ certified
paper—one small step in DK's
commitment to a sustainable
future. For more information go to
www.dk.com/our-green-pledge

CONTENTS

The dates in this book range from millions of years ago to just decades. Some may be followed by MYA, short for "million years ago." Other dates have BCE and CE after them. These are short for "Before the Common Era" and "Common Era". The Common Era dates from when people think Jesus Christ was born.

Where the exact date of an event is not known, "c." is used. This is short for the Latin word *circa*, meaning "around," and indicates that the date is approximate.

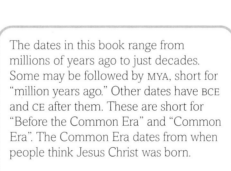

PREHISTORY

Prehistory

The period before writing was invented (just over 5,000 years ago) is known as prehistory. As there are no written records from this time, what we know of human prehistory comes from physical evidence such as fossils and tools.

The prehistory of humanity covers a vast period—it is many times longer than the whole of written human history. The first known writing was developed in North Africa and the Middle East in c. 3300–3200 BCE, but modern humans (*Homo sapiens*) have existed for around 300,000 years. Our human ancestors began to walk upright even earlier, around 6–7 million years ago.

Human origins
The ancestors of humans evolved in Africa, and around 4 million years ago the species known as *Australopithecus afarensis* moved out of the forests and into the grasslands of East Africa. The first known human species, *Homo erectus*, left Africa around 1.9 million years ago, and other species later followed. Modern humans left Africa and spread into Asia around 194,000 years ago, and by 65,000 years ago *Homo sapiens* had reached Australia. As human species spread

VENUS OF BRASSEMPOUY
Carved from mammoth ivory, this 25,000-year-old portion of a broken figurine was found in a cave in Brassempouy, France. It is one of many "Venus" figurines sculpted in Europe around this time, and is one of the earliest known realistic depictions of a human face.

around the globe, they began to create depictions of the world around them. The first artworks were created from around 45,000 years ago, and by 17,000 years ago humans had developed many of the major artistic techniques for representing the world, including painting, drawing, sculpture, and engraving.

By this time, *Homo sapiens* was the only human species left on Earth, as all other species had become extinct. About 15,000 years ago, humans reached the Americas, and with the settlement of this landmass that followed, humans now lived in all but the most hostile regions of the planet.

From hunter-gatherers to farmers
Early modern humans survived by gathering wild fruit, vegetables, and other plant foods, and by hunting wild animals. They did not settle in one place, instead moving on from a region once its resources had been picked clean, or when the herds of animals they followed migrated to new

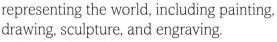

SKELETON OF "LUCY"
This partial skeleton of a female Australopithecus afarensis, *nicknamed "Lucy," is around 3.2 million years old. The structure and shape of her bones show that this species was at home both climbing trees and walking upright on the ground.*

lands. But from around 12,000 years ago, humans discovered how to grow their own crops, which led some of them to settle down in permanent villages.

As well as growing their own food, such as fruit, squashes, wheat, and rice, humans also began to farm animals for their meat and produce (such as milk, eggs, and wool). Cows were first domesticated around 10,000 years ago in Africa and the Middle East, followed over the next 5,000 years by animals such as sheep, chickens, and llamas in other parts of the world.

PLASTERED SKULL
In prehistoric Jericho, the skulls of the deceased were covered in plaster to give them new features. Many were decorated with sea shells in place of the eyes.

Belief systems also became more complex with the move to more permanent settlements. In different places around the world, worship of the sun, nature, and ancestors became common. This was partly because successful farming relied on the cycles of the natural world, and partly because people now needed a way to dispose of their dead far away from living areas. In many places, large stone structures known as megaliths (meaning "great stones") were constructed, which acted either as religious sites or as tombs for the dead.

FRUIT OF THE FIG TREE
There is evidence of fig trees being planted in West Asia as early as 11,200 years ago, making the fig one of the earliest plants to be cultivated.

The end of prehistory

Not all peoples around the world had settled down in villages and towns by around 5,000 years ago. Many continued to live at least a partly nomadic lifestyle of hunting and gathering, and some cultures still do so today. Similarly, writing did not develop in all places at once, so prehistory ended at different times around the world.

Settling down

As many people moved from a hunter-gatherer lifestyle to farming, communities settled in villages, which eventually grew into towns. Some of the earliest were Jericho in modern-day Palestine around 11,000 years ago, and Çatalhöyük in modern-day Turkey around 9,500 years ago. New technologies developed in early towns that would not have been practical for wandering bands of hunter-gatherers. People began to weave clothes on large looms, and to craft pottery for storage.

KOREAN DOLMEN
A dolmen is a type of megalith in which one stone is placed on top of smaller upright stones. The Korean peninsula is home to more than 30,000 dolmen, about 40 percent of all dolmen in the world.

Becoming human

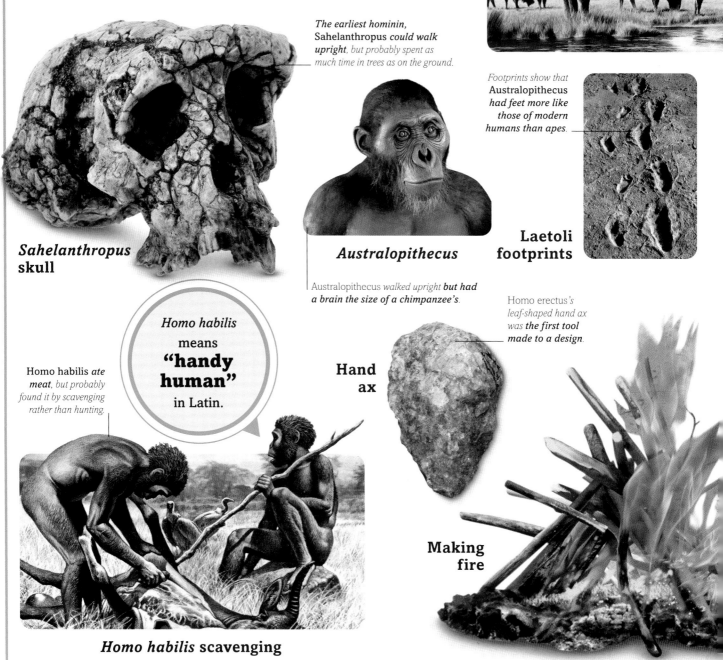

The earliest hominin, Sahelanthropus *could walk upright, but probably spent as much time in trees as on the ground.*

Footprints show that Australopithecus *had feet more like those of modern humans than apes.*

Laetoli footprints

Sahelanthropus skull

Australopithecus

Australopithecus *walked upright* **but had a brain the size of a chimpanzee's.**

Homo habilis means **"handy human"** in Latin.

Homo habilis *ate* **meat,** *but probably found it by scavenging rather than hunting.*

Hand ax

Homo erectus's *leaf-shaped hand ax was* **the first tool made to a design.**

Making fire

***Homo habilis* scavenging**

Modern humans and their recent ancestors, together known as hominins, evolved from apes in Africa. By about 6 MYA (million years ago) hominins were walking upright. Over time, they developed bigger brains and learned to make tools and fire. Many left Africa and spread across the world.

The earliest known hominin, **Sahelanthropus**, lived about 7–6 MYA in the forests of Africa. Around 4 MYA, the upright walking apes **Australopithecus** spread across the grasslands of East Africa. Walking upright helped them see farther, kept them cooler, and freed their hands to carry and throw. By 3.3 MYA, hominins were making the first stone tools. Larger

Homo heidelbergensis hunting wild cattle

Homo heidelbergensis *was the first known hominin to make wooden spears and used them to hunt wild animals.*

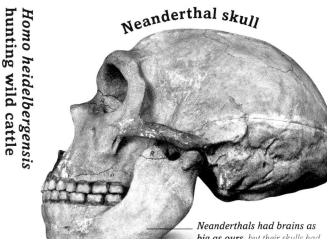

Neanderthal skull

Neanderthals had brains as big as ours, but their skulls had striking ridges on their brows.

Nicknamed "the Hobbit", Homo floresiensis *was just 3 ft 3 in (1 m) tall.*

Homo floresiensis

About a million years ago, Homo erectus *started using fire to cook meat, keep warm, and drive away wild animals.*

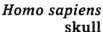

Unlike earlier hominins, modern humans have high skulls and no brow ridges.

Homo sapiens skull

BURYING THE DEAD

Neanderthals may have been the first hominins to bury their dead, placing them in caves with offerings such as flowers. Below is the skeleton of a Neanderthal man, who was buried in Israel 60,000 years ago.

Larger hominins evolved over time until 1.9 MYA, when **Homo erectus** reached the body size of modern humans. *Homo erectus* invented the leaf-shaped **hand ax**, learned to control fire, and began to migrate to Asia. About 700,000 years ago, **Homo heidelbergensis** moved into Europe and built the first known shelters. They evolved into the **Neanderthals**, who wore animal-skin clothing and buried their dead. Our species, **Homo sapiens**, appeared in Africa about 300,000 years ago. Archaeologists are still discovering previously unknown hominins, such as **Homo floresiensis**, who lived in Flores, Indonesia, around 100,000–50,000 years ago.

Peopling the world

*Scientific studies have proven that **modern humans and Neanderthals intermingled and had children with each other**.*

Diprotodon

Bone needle

*The invention of the bone needle around 30,000 years ago **allowed people to sew well-fitted clothing**.*

Clothing was decorated using different types of material, such as these mammoth beads found in a 30,000-year-old burial site at Sungir, Russia.

Meeting Neanderthals

Clothes

*In Australia, people hunted herds of **Diprotodon**, a giant wombat, that became extinct around 44,000 BCE.*

The boomerang, which can be seen in Australian rock art from around 20,000 years ago, has a curved design and the shape of its surface allows it to fly through the air with great precision.

Boomerang

🔍 OUT OF AFRICA

Early population movements were made during a period when sea levels were lower than they are today. People could wade across the Red Sea from Africa to Asia, make a short sea journey to reach Australia, and follow a land bridge to get to North America. This map shows how modern humans spread around the globe over thousands of years.

KEY

Land during low sea levels	194,000–88,000 years ago	80,000–45,000 years ago
65,000 years ago	50,000 years ago	23,000–15,000 years ago	14,000–10,000 years ago

GREENLAND

Beringia

Siberia

Rocky Mountains

Ushki complex

NORTH AMERICA

EUROPE Kostenki

Mal'ta

• Pestera cu Oase

Jebel Irhoud

ASIA

• Tianyuan Cave

Pacific Ocean

Clovis

Sahara Desert

AFRICA

Balangoda

Atlantic Ocean

Indian Ocean

SAHUL (AUSTRALIA)

SOUTH AMERICA

Andes

Fell's Cave

Hunters built shelters using mammoth bones covered with mammoth hides (skin) on the icy steppes of Asia.

Mammoth-bone house

Modern humans, or *Homo sapiens*, evolved around 300,000 years ago in Africa. About 194,000 years ago, they began leaving Africa in a series of waves. They traveled on foot, and later by boat, looking for new food sources. Eventually, they reached most parts of Earth, from the Arctic to remote Pacific islands.

After leaving Africa, modern humans first kept to warm regions, going east as they followed the coast of Asia. In Asia, they met other hominins (see pp. 10–11), including the **Neanderthals**. The earliest boat journeys were undertaken by people from Asia who reached Australia about 65,000 years ago. Here, they invented specialized tools, such as the

Lion Man of Hohlenstein-Stadel

Around 12 in (30 cm) tall, this sculpture is carved from mammoth ivory and **depicts a humanlike figure with the head of a lion**.

Animal migrations

Many modern humans reached far-off regions while following migrating herds of animals, which they kept close to as a source of food.

First art

Drawn c. 45,500 years ago, this painting of a pig in Indonesia is believed to be the **oldest known cave painting of an animal**.

Hunters of the Clovis culture of North America **made beautiful leaf-shaped spear points from stone**.

Clovis spear point

It is thought that it took around **400 hours** to carve the Lion Man.

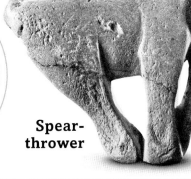

Spear-thrower

This carving of a mammoth, made from a reindeer antler, is a spear-thrower—**a tool used to throw spears with a great force**.

One of the earliest **types of cave painting** was made by people spraying paint over their hands using hollow bird bones, as seen on the walls of Cueva de las Manos in Argentina.

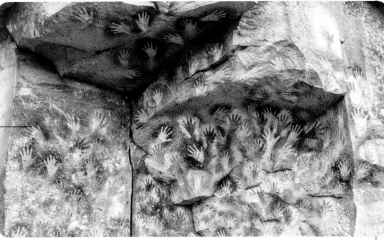

Hand stencils

boomerang, and found new types of animals to hunt, including the **Diprotodon**. The development of warm clothing allowed humans to move north into the colder parts of Europe and Asia. They used **spear-throwers** to hunt mammoths for food, making **mammoth-bone houses** and beads from mammoth ivory. From 45,000 years ago, people in different parts of the world began creating the **first art**, including cave paintings of animals, **hand stencils**, and sculptures. Between 23,000 and 15,000 years ago, humans began moving to the Americas. One of the earliest cultures was the Clovis, whose people left evidence such as **spear points**.

SETTLING AUSTRALIA
More than 60,000 years ago, people from Southeast Asia traveled to and settled in the continent now known as Australia. They were the First Nations Australians, a people who created a unique way of life and a millennia-long culture. The long history of their settlement of Australia can be seen in their art, such as in this cave painting from Mount Borradaile, Northern Territory, Australia.

The First Nations Australians mostly settled along the coastlines or inland along river valleys of the continent. They carefully observed their new environment to find the best ways to survive, and moved from place to place according to the seasons. These people have always seen themselves as caretakers of the land they live on, and have felt a duty to live responsibly. Their beliefs and ideas have been passed on from generation to generation through a rich culture of sharing stories, and through artwork at their sacred sites across Australia. Their rock art—often colored using pigments made from crushed minerals—is among the oldest in the world.

First farmers

Wheat

Unlike wild wheat, which shatters when ripe, **the grains of domesticated wheat need to be harvested.**

First cultivated in China, rice is grown in flooded fields, and each plant must be individually planted.

Wet rice farming

Sorghum, which can resist both dry spells and heavy rain, is the perfect crop for Africa's climate.

Sorghum

The first farmers harvested grains using flint sickles with wooden handles.

Women spent long hours grinding grain using a **quern**, a long, flat stone with an upper grinding stone.

Quern stone

Mouflon

Flint sickle

Maize

Farmers in Mesoamerica kept planting only the best examples of a wild grass called teosinte **until it eventually developed into maize.**

In ancient India, oxen were **used to pull carts,** as shown in this model from Mohenjo-Daro in modern-day Pakistan.

Pulling carts

Through domestication, **the mouflon lost its long horns and developed thicker wool on its body.**

Alpaca

In the Peruvian Andes, people domesticated **alpacas** for meat and wool.

Dating from c. 7400–6200 BCE, **Çatalhöyük, in modern-day Turkey, is one of the world's oldest towns.**

Çatalhöyük

Around 12,000 years ago, people in the Middle East stopped living as hunter-gatherers, and began to produce their own food by farming. They planted seeds and controlled the breeding of wild animals. The new way of life was later adopted in several other parts of the world.

Plants and animals changed greatly as a result of domestication (being brought under human control). The earliest crops in the Middle East were grasses, such as **wheat** and barley. Domesticated plants have bigger seeds than wild ones, and the seeds can no longer be spread by the wind and need to be planted. Animals that were easy to control were the first to be

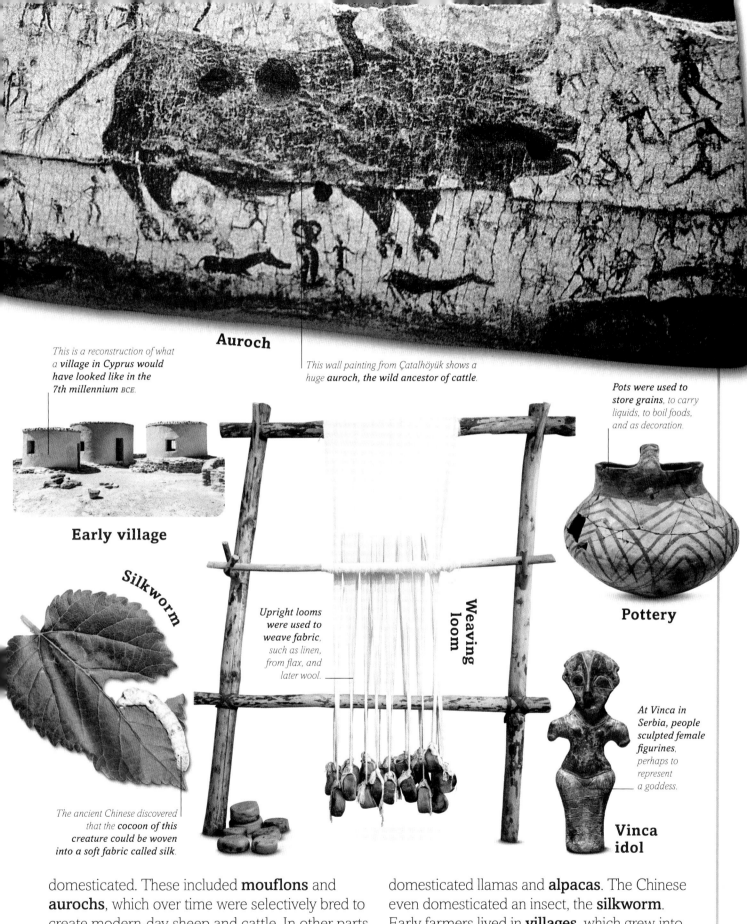

Auroch

*This wall painting from Çatalhöyük shows a huge **auroch, the wild ancestor of cattle.***

*This is a reconstruction of what a **village in Cyprus would have looked like** in the 7th millennium BCE.*

Early village

Silkworm

*The ancient Chinese discovered that the **cocoon of this creature could be woven** into a soft fabric called silk.*

Upright looms were used to weave fabric, such as linen, from flax, and later wool.

Weaving loom

Pots were used to store grains, to carry liquids, to boil foods, and as decoration.

Pottery

At Vinca in Serbia, people sculpted female figurines, perhaps to represent a goddess.

Vinca idol

domesticated. These included **mouflons** and **aurochs**, which over time were selectively bred to create modern-day sheep and cattle. In other parts of the world, different crops and animals were domesticated. **Rice** was grown in China, **sorghum** in sub-Saharan Africa, **maize** in Mesoamerica, and potatoes in South America. In Peru, people domesticated llamas and **alpacas**. The Chinese even domesticated an insect, the **silkworm**. Early farmers lived in **villages**, which grew into towns, one of the earliest being **Çatalhöyük** in Turkey. Settled life led to new technology, such as **weaving looms**, **pottery**, and **quern stones**.

After the Ice Age

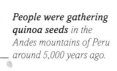

People were gathering **quinoa seeds** in the Andes mountains of Peru around 5,000 years ago.

Quinoa seeds

This rock painting in South Africa shows people hunting deer with bows and arrows.

Hunter-gatherers roasted hazelnuts to improve their flavor and to preserve them.

Hazelnuts

Prehistoric paddle

This 9,500-year-old **hazel-wood paddle** was found among the remains of a prehistoric settlement at Ulkestrup Lyng in Denmark.

Bows and arrows

Stone spear points have been discovered among bison bones, suggesting they were used to hunt the animals.

Folsom spear point

This reconstruction of a prehistoric **house** at the Archaeolink Prehistory Park in Scotland allowed visitors to see how people lived thousands of years ago.

Microlith

Microliths are tiny stone blades that were **tied** to handles to make sickles and scrapers.

Reconstructed prehistoric dwelling

About 20,000 to 15,000 years ago, most of Earth's northern regions were covered in ice. Around 14,000 to 12,000 years ago, the climate grew warmer and wetter. As ice melted, sea levels rose, rivers appeared, and forests replaced grassland. People's lives changed as many new sources of food became available.

As the temperature and landscape changed, mammoths and other big game animals that lived in colder regions started dying out, transforming how hunter-gatherers lived. Big game hunting only continued in North America, where people of the central plains, such as the **Folsom** culture, followed bison herds and hunted them with spears. However,

Bone necklace

This necklace, made from bone beads and the shells of sea mollusks, was **created by the Natufian culture in southwest Asia c. 11,000 BCE.**

Antler headdress

Antler headdresses may have been used in **religious rituals**.

Antler headdresses, made by drilling eye holes into deer skulls, have been found at Star Carr, a prehistoric site in the UK.

Dating back to 10,000 BCE, the structure at Göbekli Tepe is believed to be **the oldest place of worship constructed by humans.**

Göbekli Tepe

Jomon cooking vessel

Jomon potters made decorated pots for cooking over bonfires in the open air.

People from Jomon Japan made many small clay figurines of women, perhaps representing goddesses.

Jomon ritual figurine

in Europe, Asia, and Africa, people began hunting smaller forest animals, especially deer, using **bows and arrows**. New foods also became part of the human diet, such as **quinoa seeds** and **hazelnuts**. Dugout boats powered by **paddles** allowed people to travel over water and catch fish using harpoons. People were so successful at gathering wild food

that they began settling down, forming lasting villages in some places. Some of the world's first **pottery** was made by settled hunter-gatherers during the Jomon period in Japan. Even the world's first known stone building was set up by hunter-gatherers at **Göbekli Tepe**, in present-day Turkey.

MEGALITHS
Once ancient people lived settled lives, some began to build the world's first large monuments, called megaliths (Greek for "big stone"). These include standing stones—set up singly or arranged in rows or circles—and dolmens, which were stone tombs built in the shape of a table. Megaliths can be found around the world, from this stone circle at Stonehenge, UK, to the dolmens in the Korean peninsula.

The purpose of standing stones remains a mystery. Like dolmens, they may have been set up in honor of the dead. The structures at Stonehenge were built between 3000 and 1500 BCE and may have been used for religious rituals. While most megaliths used unshaped stones, the largest stones at Stonehenge are carefully shaped. These were set up as trilithons (two upright stones with a horizontal one on top). The placement of the stones suggests that they are connected to the sun's movement—some of them frame the midsummer sunrise and midwinter sunset. Today, many people still visit Stonehenge at midsummer to celebrate the sunrise.

Metalworking

*Ancient Egyptian craftworkers **used wooden mallets and copper chisels** to carve stone.*

Egyptian mallet and chisel

Bull-shaped ornament

*This small gold ornament is part of a **treasure trove from c. 4500 BCE, found in Varna, Bulgaria**.*

The dancing girl

Measuring 4 in (10.5 cm) tall, the dancing girl was found in 1926 in the ruins of Mohenjo-Daro (in modern-day Pakistan).

The dancing girl is one of the **oldest** bronze sculptures ever found.

Sanxingdui bronze

Statues from Sanxingdui, China, have a green crust called verdigris, which forms when bronze is exposed to air and moisture.

Hittite silver rhyton

Rhytons are ornate vessels, usually in the shape of animals, that were used to pour or drink wine during feasts.

At different times around the world, people learned to use metals. Unlike stone, metal could be molded into different shapes, and melted and reused. Rare metals like gold and silver became a new form of wealth. As techniques improved, people learned to work with harder metals, such as bronze and iron.

Metalworking began in western Asia, around c. 4500 BCE, with metals such as copper and gold. Molten copper was poured into molds to make tools such as **chisels**, while gold could be hammered into thin sheets to make decorative items. From c. 3500 BCE, metalworkers began adding a small amount of the metal tin to copper

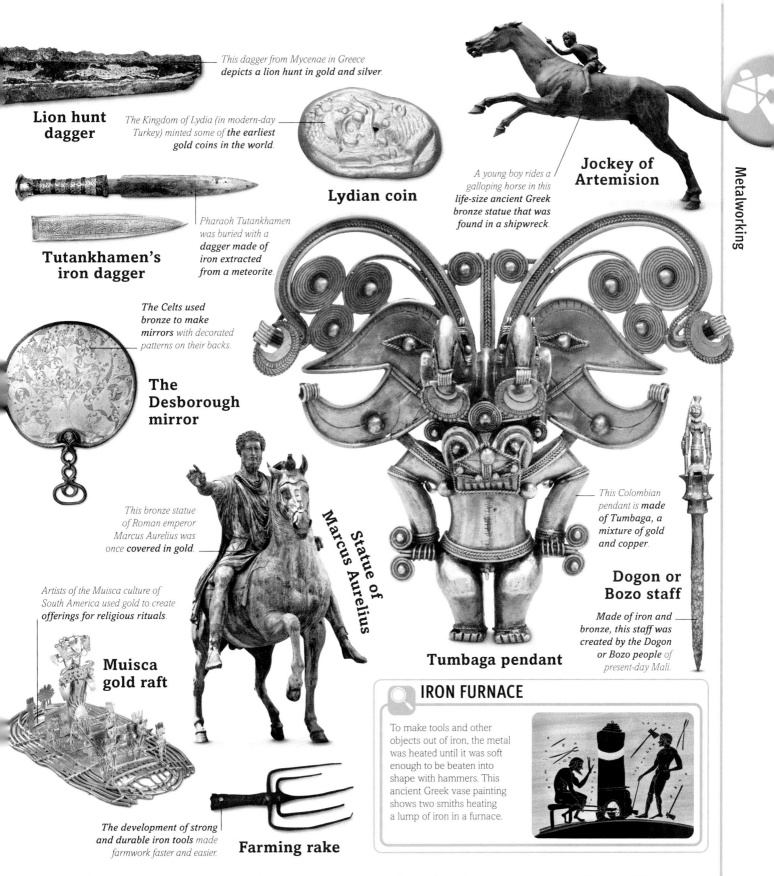

Lion hunt dagger

This dagger from Mycenae in Greece depicts a lion hunt in gold and silver.

*The Kingdom of Lydia (in modern-day Turkey) minted some of **the earliest gold coins in the world**.*

Lydian coin

Jockey of Artemision

A young boy rides a galloping horse in this life-size ancient Greek bronze statue that was found in a shipwreck.

Tutankhamen's iron dagger

*Pharaoh Tutankhamen was buried with a **dagger made of iron** extracted from a meteorite.*

*The Celts used **bronze to make mirrors** with decorated patterns on their backs.*

The Desborough mirror

Statue of Marcus Aurelius

*This bronze statue of Roman emperor Marcus Aurelius was once **covered in gold**.*

*This Colombian pendant is **made of Tumbaga**, a mixture of gold and copper.*

Dogon or Bozo staff

Made of iron and bronze, this staff was created by the Dogon or Bozo people of present-day Mali.

Tumbaga pendant

Artists of the Muisca culture of South America used gold to create offerings for religious rituals.

Muisca gold raft

IRON FURNACE

To make tools and other objects out of iron, the metal was heated until it was soft enough to be beaten into shape with hammers. This ancient Greek vase painting shows two smiths heating a lump of iron in a furnace.

The development of strong and durable iron tools made farmwork faster and easier.

Farming rake

to make bronze, a harder material. Bronze was used for making weapons, such as the ancient Greek **lion hunt dagger**, as well as for sculptures, such as the Indus Valley **dancing girl** and the Chinese **Sanxingdui bronzes**. From 1200 BCE, people in many parts of the world began working with iron. A hard metal, iron had to be beaten to be

shaped, and over time came to be used for weapons and tools, such as **farming rakes**. Although people in the ancient Americas rarely used hard metals, they prized gold, silver, and copper—using them to create works of art, such as the **Tumbaga pendant** and the **Muisca gold raft**.

THE ANCIENT WORLD

The Ancient World

As villages grew into towns and then into cities, civilizations began to arise. The first emerged in the Middle East and Egypt, but eventually great city-based cultures sprang up independently in many areas around the world.

The first known cities were built more than 5,000 years ago, close to rivers that supported farming on a large scale. In Mesopotamia (in modern-day Iraq), cities were built near the Tigris and Euphrates rivers, while in Egypt the fertile land along the banks of the Nile was the site of the ancient Egyptian civilization. Early cities within the same region traded with each other but also competed for land and resources, leading to war. As cities increased their territory and influence, great empires were born.

THE ROSETTA STONE
The ability to read ancient Egyptian was lost until 1799, with the discovery of the Rosetta Stone. This fragment was carved with the same text written in two Egyptian writing systems—hieroglyphics and Demotic—as well as Ancient Greek. Reading the Greek text allowed translators to decipher the Egyptian writing systems.

Early civilization
Mesopotamians and ancient Egyptians developed many of the first features of civilization, such as rule by a monarch, a code of laws, and organized religion. They were also the first cultures to develop writing. Ancient Egypt existed for more than 3,000 years, but it was not the only ancient African civilization. During this time, African kingdoms south of the Sahara such as the Kush and Nok kingdoms rose and fell.

LAOZI
According to legend, philosopher Laozi was the founder of Daoism, an important philosophical and religious tradition that sprang up in China in the 6th century BCE. Daoism teaches a life of harmony with nature by following the dao ("the Way").

Eastern beliefs
Another civilization that would last for thousands of years emerged in East Asia during this period. Developing from a small kingdom, China eventually became a large and powerful state united under the rule of an emperor in 221 BCE. Along the way, many of the philosophies that laid the foundations of Chinese belief, such as Confucianism and Daoism, first appeared.

In ancient India, another major religious and philosophical tradition emerged in the 6th century BCE—Buddhism. The teachings of Buddhism spread throughout much of the Indian subcontinent, influencing empires such as the Mauryans and the Kushans. Over the next thousand years, Buddhism reached as far as China, Southeast Asia, Korea, and Japan. Eventually, Buddhist thought became influential in belief systems across the whole of Asia.

The Mediterranean and Europe

A different story emerged in Europe and the lands surrounding the Mediterranean Sea, which were home to a series of civilizations with their own beliefs and ways of thinking. Around the Mediterranean, civilizations such as the Minoans, Phoenicians, and the ancient Greeks sprang up, all influencing each other through trade and conflict. To the north, the Celts also had close links with this Mediterranean world.

But in the 3rd century BCE, a new power, Rome, began to expand its territory and spread its influence across the region. By the time it reached its greatest extent in 117 CE, the Roman Empire encompassed all the lands that bordered the Mediterranean Sea, from modern-day Spain to the coasts of North Africa, as well as much of western Europe. The western portion of the Roman Empire gradually fell into decline in the following centuries, finally collapsing in the 5th century CE when Germanic peoples invaded from the north and east.

ZAPOTEC GOLD

For many Mesoamerican cultures, gold was a precious material used to craft objects that showed off a person's wealth and power, such as this elaborate earring from the Zapotec civilization.

Cultures around the globe

The civilizations of ancient Africa, Asia, and Europe were connected to each other by overland trade routes or relatively short voyages by sea. But on the other side of vast oceans, the civilizations of the ancient Americas developed without any contact with the rest of the world. The earliest American civilization, the Norte Chico, emerged around 5,000 years ago in modern-day Peru in South America. Ancient societies such as the Zapotec and Maya flourished in Mesoamerica, a region that included modern-day Mexico and much of Central America. Further north, Indigenous peoples such as the Adena left their mark on the landscape itself, creating huge mounds in the shape of animals as part of their religious traditions.

Many great civilizations rose up throughout the ancient world, and their influence can still be felt today. But most of these societies, particularly in Europe and Asia, had fallen into decline by the end of the 6th century CE, thanks to disease, power struggles, and invasion.

ANCIENT ATHENS

A powerful city-state in ancient Greece, Athens had a huge influence on Western civilization. It was the birthplace of democracy in Europe, developed many of the features of modern drama and theater, and its thinkers laid the foundations for much of Western philosophy.

Mesopotamia

Priest-king

Made of a copper alloy, this figurine is thought to depict a priest-king in Uruk, the oldest Sumerian city.

Accounts for food supplies are written in cuneiform on this **clay tablet from around 2800** BCE.

Ram in a Thicket

Despite its name, this statue—made of gold, shell, and lapis lazuli—shows a grazing goat.

Kings and queens were buried with games to play in the afterlife.

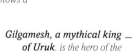

Royal Game of Ur

Gilgamesh, a mythical king of Uruk, is the hero of the world's oldest surviving story.

This Akkadian bronze sculpture of a king is thought to be of Sargon, who founded Akkad, the world's first empire.

Sargon of Akkad

Cuneiform

A box decorated with a mosaic, the Standard of Ur shows a palace feast.

Standard of Ur

The top of this stele shows Shamash, the god of justice, presenting objects that signify the law to King Hammurabi of Babylon.

Code of Hammurabi

Gilgamesh

Mesopotamia means "land between two rivers" in Ancient Greek, as it was located near the Tigris and Euphrates rivers (in present-day Iraq). The world's first cities appeared here 6,000 years ago, and many features of civilization, such as religion, laws, and warfare, began in Mesopotamia.

Mesopotamian civilization began in a land called Sumer. By c. 3300 BCE, there were around 12 Sumerian cities, each led by a **priest-king** who was said to rule on behalf of a local god. In the city of Ur, kings and queens were buried in royal tombs, with treasures such as **Queen Puabi's headdress**, the **Ram in a Thicket** statue, and the

Ziggurat of Ur

Made of mud bricks, the ziggurat was built in a temple complex at the center of the city.

Statues of Lamassu, a type of guardian spirit with a human head and winged bull body, protected all Assyrian palaces.

Assyrian Lamassu

Palace feasts were accompanied by music played by harpists, as seen on this Babylonian terra-cotta relief.

Babylonian harpist

The headdress is made of 20 gold leaves, two strings of lapis lazuli, and a large gold comb.

Decorated with blue glazed tiles showing bulls and dragons, the Ishtar Gate was built in Babylon by King Nebuchadnezzar II around 575 BCE.

Ishtar Gate

🔍 MESOPOTAMIAN EMPIRES

King Sargon of Akkad, who conquered Sumer around 2330 BCE, was the first in a series of empire builders. The Akkadians were followed by the Babylonians c. 1900 BCE, and then the Assyrians by 950 BCE. The Assyrians ruled an empire stretching from present-day Egypt to western Iran. But they were overthrown by the Babylonians, who created a second Babylonian Empire around 614 BCE.

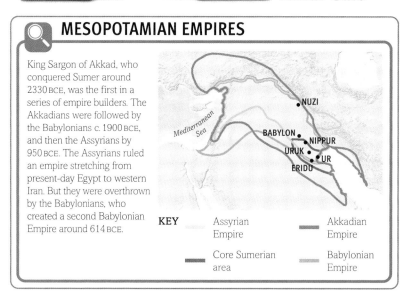

NUZI
Mediterranean Sea
BABYLON
NIPPUR
URUK
UR
ERIDU

KEY

| | Assyrian Empire | | Akkadian Empire |
| | Core Sumerian area | | Babylonian Empire |

Queen Puabi's headdress

Standard of Ur. Sumerians invented **cuneiform** writing, later used to write down stories, the oldest known being the epic of **Gilgamesh**. Sumer was conquered by **Sargon of Akkad** around 2330 BCE. The Akkadians built massive temple structures known as **ziggurats**. The city of Babylon later rose to become the capital of the first Babylonian Empire, which is known for the **Code of Hammurabi**, a set of laws established around 1750 BCE by King Hammurabi. Then the Assyrians conquered the region. After them a second Babylonian Empire arose, during which the city's famous **Ishtar Gate** was built.

Ancient warfare

Ur spearhead

*Spears with sharp metal heads were **used by foot soldiers from Ur in ancient Mesopotamia**.*

Chinese dagger-ax

Chinese foot soldiers fought with bronze dagger-axes that were mounted on long poles.

War elephants could trample and terrify soldiers and horses on the battlefield, as seen on this carving from Sanchi, India.

Indian war elephants

Nubia, a region along the Nile River, was known as the "land of the bow" *because its armies had the most skilled archers at that time.*

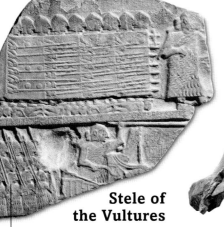

Nubian archers

Stele of the Vultures

This stele shows the victorious marching army of Lagash carrying spears and shields.

Greek hoplite

*Persian kings were guarded by elite **archers** known as the Immortals.*

*Greek hoplites were **named after their big, round shield,** the hoplon.*

Persian archers

Warfare has been part of human life since the rise of the first civilizations, when cities fought each other over land and resources. The desire for military victory led to many technological advancements, such as the invention of chariots, warships, and stronger, lighter armor.

The first recorded wars were fought from c. 2700 BCE by the rival cities of Mesopotamia. One of these, the battle between the cities of Umma and Lagash, was recorded on a limestone relief—the **Stele of the Vultures**. Most ancient wars were fought by foot

NAVAL WARFARE

Though ancient warships had sails for long-distance travel, they were usually rowed in battle. Ancient Greek warships, called triremes, had three banks of rowers and a battering ram at the prow. The aim was to sink an enemy ship by smashing its sides with the ram.

A single square sail

Battering ram

Egyptian pharaoh Tutankhamen shoots arrows while riding his chariot into battle in this decoration from a panel on a chest.

Egyptian chariot

Japanese warriors in the 6th century CE wore helmets and carried swords, as can be seen in this Kofun pottery figurine.

Japanese warrior

The nomadic tribes of the Scythians were expert riders, and their horseback warriors were feared throughout Central Asia.

Scythian warrior

Roman legionnaires wore flexible armor made of overlapping curved iron plates and a Gallic helmet for protecting the face, and they used a steel sword for close combat.

War clubs of the Moche culture of Peru were blunt at one end and pointed at the other, allowing them to be used as a club or a spear.

Roman legionnaire armor and weapon

Moche warrior

Qin Dynasty Chinese soldiers wore armor made of small leather or metal plates.

soldiers, such as the **Nubian archers** and Chinese infantry wielding **dagger-axes**. From 2000 BCE, the use of horse-drawn **chariots** made armies more mobile. In central Eurasia, the horseback **Scythian warriors** were a constant threat to settled populations, while in South Asia, rulers used **war elephants** to crush their enemies in battle. Mounted soldiers gave an army a strong advantage, but so did training and organization. In the 5th century BCE, skilled **hoplite** soldiers were able to defeat the more numerous Persian forces. Some of the most disciplined and well-trained ancient soldiers were **Roman legionnaires**, foot soldiers who helped build one of the largest empires in history.

Ancient Egypt

Life in Egypt depended on the Nile River,
which flooded every year, leaving fertile black
silt where farmers could plant their crops.

Nile River

First Pharaoh

This stele depicts
Pharaoh Narmer
wearing the
white crown of
Upper Egypt, the
southern kingdom.

Statues of
scribes have
rolls of fat,
showing that they
did not have to
do physical work.

Scribe

The biggest
pyramids, at Giza,
are guarded by a
great statue of
a sphinx.

The sphinx has the **body of a lion** and the **head of a pharaoh**.

Pyramids

A kneeling priest
plays music as a way
of worshipping the sun
god, Re Horakhty, who
has the head of a hawk
wearing a solar disk.

Music

Egyptians usually
traveled on the Nile River,
by boat, heading north with
the current, or sailing south
using sails and oars.

Ancient Egyptian boat

Ancient Egypt was one of the world's longest-lasting civilizations, thriving for more than 3,000 years after its foundation in the 31st century BCE. Throughout this period, Egyptians spoke the same language and followed a similar yearly routine that was based on the flooding of the Nile River.

Egyptian civilization developed on the banks of the **Nile River**, where the land was fertile. Deserts on each side of the river protected Egypt from foreign invasions, allowing the civilization to flourish. Most Egyptians were farmers, whose lives were organized by a class of educated **scribes**, who could read and write. The Egyptians worshipped

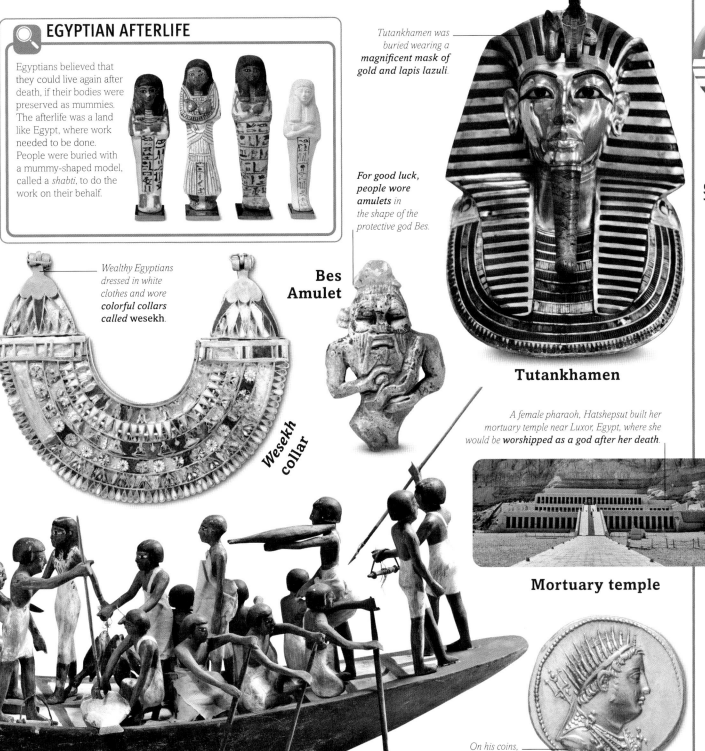

EGYPTIAN AFTERLIFE

Egyptians believed that they could live again after death, if their bodies were preserved as mummies. The afterlife was a land like Egypt, where work needed to be done. People were buried with a mummy-shaped model, called a *shabti*, to do the work on their behalf.

Tutankhamen was buried wearing a **magnificent mask of gold and lapis lazuli**.

For good luck, people wore **amulets** *in the shape of the protective god Bes.*

Bes Amulet

Tutankhamen

Wealthy Egyptians dressed in white clothes and wore **colorful collars called** wesekh.

Wesekh collar

A female pharaoh, Hatshepsut built her mortuary temple near Luxor, Egypt, where she would be **worshipped as a god after her death**.

Mortuary temple

On his coins, Ptolemy IV (221–205 BCE) was **shown as a Greek ruler**.

Ptolemy IV Philopator

many gods, such as Re, Horus, and **Bes**, as well as their pharaohs, who built **mortuary temples** for themselves. Originally there were two kingdoms, Upper and Lower Egypt—which were said to have been united by Narmer, the **first pharaoh**. During the Old Kingdom period (c. 2686–2181 BCE), pharaohs were buried in great stone tombs called **pyramids**. Later pharaohs of the New Kingdom (c. 1550–1069 BCE), such as **Tutankhamen**, were buried in rock-cut tombs in the desert, west of the capital, Thebes. The last pharaohs, ruling from 322–31 BCE, were Macedonians from Greece— a line of kings all called **Ptolemy**, and one female pharaoh, Cleopatra.

Gods and religion

*The snake-tongued Cocijo, god of rain, thunder, and lightning, was **an important deity of the Zapotec people of Mesoamerica**.*

The Egyptian goddess Isis holds her son, Horus, the sky god.

Isis and Horus

Baal Hammon was the chief god of the ancient North African empire of Carthage, in what is now Tunisia.

Baal Hammon

*The ancient Mesopotamians **left statuettes of worshippers in temples to pray on their behalf**.*

Mesopotamian worship figure

*The face on this carved bowl from the Chavin culture of Peru looks human, but its **jaguar fangs suggest that it may be a religious figure**.*

Cocijo

Chavin carving

Religious beliefs have changed over the course of time. The first human communities usually worshipped natural phenomena or their ancestors, while later ones had many different gods with specialized roles. This was followed by religions based on religious texts or the teachings of a spiritual leader.

Early civilizations worshipped gods that could help them flourish, such as **Baal Hammon** and **Cocijo** who provided rain for crops, or gods that could assist during times of war. Ancient gods often had their own forms of royalty as well as families and relationships, much like humans. Mother and son **Isis and Horus** were among

The Dome of the Rock is a mosque that sits on Temple Mount—*an area in Jerusalem that is sacred in Judaism, Christianity, and Islam.*

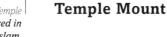
Temple Mount

Chinese Daoists worship the Jade Emperor, who has a whole court of deities working as his officials.

Jade Emperor

Buddhists worship through meditation, and depictions of the Buddha usually show him meditating.

Buddha sculpture, China

Vikings in Scandinavia wore amulets that looked like the hammer of Thor, the god of thunder, for good luck.

In the Japanese religion of Shintoism, a kitsune is a fox who acts as a messenger for the kami *(nature spirits).*

Thor

A symbol of the ancient Persian religion of Zoroastrianism, the winged Faravahar represents the immortal human soul.

Faravahar

Kitsune

Ganesha

The elephant-headed Hindu god Ganesha is the patron of wisdom, writing, and art.

Eshu

Zeus, Greek god of the sky, was shown holding thunderbolts, which he threw down from the sky when he was angry.

This Italian mosaic shows Jesus Christ as a Roman soldier, trampling animals that represent evil.

Representing ancestors, hei-tiki are small pendants worn for protection by the Māori people of New Zealand.

Sculptures of Eshu show him with elongated headdresses, and occasionally playing a flute.

Zeus

Jesus Christ

Hei-tiki

Egypt's most important deities, while the Chinese god **Jade Emperor** and the Greek **Zeus** ruled over a large number of gods. Some gods had a unique appearance, such as **Ganesha** from the Indian subcontinent. In Africa, the Yoruba people worship powerful *orisha* (spiritual entities), such as **Eshu**, who act as mediators between gods and humans. Some belief systems spread far beyond their place of origin to become world religions. These include Buddhism, which follows the teachings of the Buddha, and Judaism, Christianity, and Islam, which are based on belief in just one god and in sacred books.

TEMPLE WORSHIP
In the ancient world, a temple was seen as the house of a god, whose statue was kept in an inner room, the shrine. Usually only priests and priestesses could enter this sacred space, while ordinary people worshipped outside the shrine. The ancient Egyptian rulers, or pharaohs, built many temples for their gods—the largest of which is the Karnak Temple Complex, near Luxor in Egypt.

An important ancient Egyptian temple was that of Amun-Re, king of the gods, on the eastern side of the Nile River at Karnak. Founded around 2000 BCE, it was enlarged by a series of pharaohs over the next 2,000 years. The ancient Egyptians believed that their gods, like humans, had physical needs. Each morning, priests would wash the statue of a god, and give it a new set of clothes, fresh makeup, and food. Ordinary Egyptians had to provide the temple with food offerings, which was a form of taxation. The people only saw the statues of the gods during festivals, when they were taken out on processions.

Ancient China

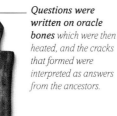

Questions were written on oracle bones which were then heated, and the cracks that formed were interpreted as answers from the ancestors.

Shang Dynasty oracle bone

Zhou ceremonial bronze vessel

Cauldron-like bronze vessels were used to serve grain and meat during rituals.

Xiongnu horse rider

Under the Zhou, each state had its own currency, such as these spade-shaped coins.

Spade-shaped Zhou coin

Confucius

Qin Shi Huangdi

The Zhou Dynasty faced frequent attacks by the nomadic Xiongnu warriors, who lived in the plains to the north of China.

Ceremonial bronze vessels of the Spring and Autumn period were quite elaborate, and often shaped like animals.

Spring and Autumn period wine vessel

The philosopher Confucius, who lived during the Spring and Autumn period, advised Zhou rulers to treat their subjects kindly.

After uniting the warring states, the Qin ruler took the title Qin Shi Huangdi, which means "the First Emperor of Qin (China)".

> The Qin and Han buried their dead with objects that could be used in **the afterlife**.

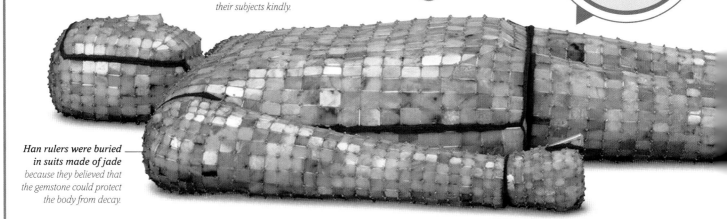

Han rulers were buried in suits made of jade because they believed that the gemstone could protect the body from decay.

From 1600 BCE to 220 CE, the region now known as China was ruled by four successive dynasties—the Shang, the Zhou, the Qin, and the Han. From a small kingdom under the Shang, China became a large, unified empire under the Qin and Han dynasties, and a powerful state in the region.

The Shang ruled over a small state in northern China from c. 1600 to 1045 BCE. Shang rulers worshipped their ancestors, using **oracle bones** to seek guidance. They were overthrown by the Zhou, who ruled over a small collection of states. The Zhou period is known for its **spade-shaped coins** and elaborate **bronze vessels**. The period from

Shang Yang

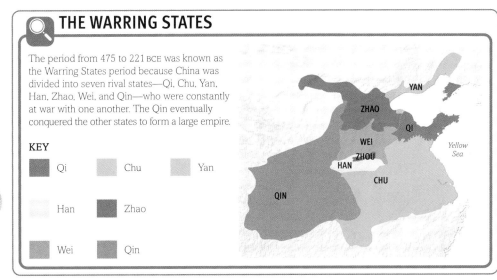

THE WARRING STATES

The period from 475 to 221 BCE was known as the Warring States period because China was divided into seven rival states—Qi, Chu, Yan, Han, Zhao, Wei, and Qin—who were constantly at war with one another. The Qin eventually conquered the other states to form a large empire.

KEY

- ■ Qi
- ■ Chu
- ■ Yan
- ■ Han
- ■ Zhao
- ■ Wei
- ■ Qin

The Qin minister Shang Yang helped create a legal system based on strict laws and harsh punishments.

Qin Shi Huangdi was buried along with more than 8,000 life-size terra-cotta warriors in a large mound-shaped tomb.

Terracotta army

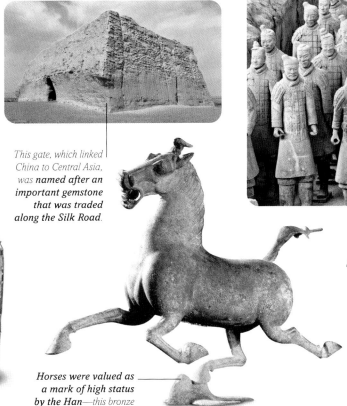

The Qin standardized coinage across their empire, introducing round coins with square holes in the center.

The Jade Gate, Silk Road

Qin coin

This gate, which linked China to Central Asia, was named after an important gemstone that was traded along the Silk Road.

An early form of the magnetic compass, invented during the Han era, used a metal spoon—balanced on a plate—to find south.

Han burial suit

Horses were valued as a mark of high status by the Han—this bronze statue was found in the tomb of an army general.

Han sculpture

Han compass

770 to 476 BCE is known as the **Spring and Autumn period**, when the Zhou gradually lost control of the states they ruled, and it was followed by the Warring States period. In 221 BCE, these states were united by **Qin Shi Huangdi**, the First Emperor of the Qin Dynasty. His rule introduced many measures to stabilize the region, such as the introduction of standardized **round coins**. The Qin Dynasty did not last long after the death of the First Emperor. It was replaced by the Han Dynasty, which expanded China into Central Asia and created a trade route to Europe that came to be known as the **Silk Road**.

Writing systems

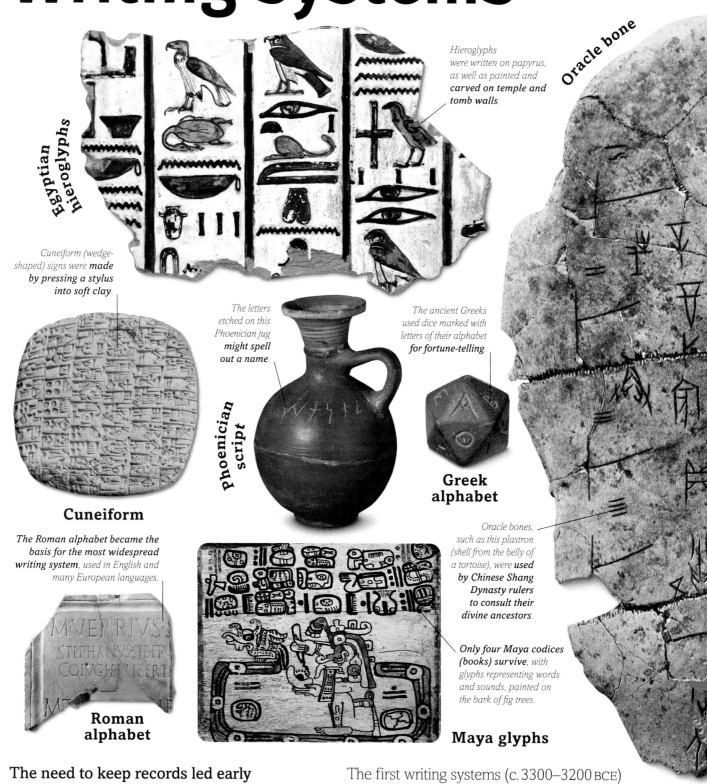

Oracle bone

Hieroglyphs were written on papyrus, as well as painted and carved on temple and tomb walls.

Egyptian hieroglyphs

Cuneiform (wedge-shaped) signs were made by pressing a stylus into soft clay.

The letters etched on this Phoenician jug might spell out a name.

Phoenician script

The ancient Greeks used dice marked with letters of their alphabet for fortune-telling.

Cuneiform

Greek alphabet

The Roman alphabet became the basis for the most widespread writing system, used in English and many European languages.

Oracle bones, such as this plastron (shell from the belly of a tortoise), were used by Chinese Shang Dynasty rulers to consult their divine ancestors.

Roman alphabet

Only four Maya codices (books) survive, with glyphs representing words and sounds, painted on the bark of fig trees.

Maya glyphs

The need to keep records led early civilizations to invent writing systems. First created to document trade and possessions, writing came to be used for many purposes, including setting down law codes, history, and literature. Its invention allowed knowledge to be collected and passed on.

The first writing systems (c. 3300–3200 BCE) were **Egyptian hieroglyphs** and Mesopotamian **cuneiform**. Both used hundreds of picture signs to stand for words and sounds. The earliest surviving Chinese writing dates from the Shang Dynasty (see pp.38–39) and was written on **oracle bones**. It had thousands of characters standing

Ethiopic script

The Ethiopic script, called Ge'ez, has 26 letters standing for consonants, with markings for vowels.

Based on Greek, the Cyrillic script was devised to translate the Bible into Slavic languages, such as Russian.

Cyrillic script

This Chinese poem from c. 1095 CE is an example of calligraphy—beautiful writing as an art form.

Chinese calligraphy

This Viking memorial stone is decorated with a serpent, whose body carries a text written in runes—letters used to write Germanic languages.

Arabic

Written from right to left, the Arabic script has 28 letters, all standing for consonants.

Germanic runes

Found on Rapa Nui, the Rongorongo glyphs have up to 600 signs, which have not yet been deciphered.

One of three writing systems used in Japan, katakana has sound signs based on Chinese characters.

Japanese katakana

Rongorongo

for words, but no sound signs. Egypt's eastern neighbors, the Canaanites of Sinai, invented the first alphabet, with just 22 letters, all of which were consonants. The Phoenicians spread this alphabet around the Mediterranean as the **Phoenician script**. This was adapted by other cultures, becoming the **Greek alphabet**, with signs added for vowels, and then, the **Roman alphabet**. Later, other alphabetic scripts were developed, including **Arabic**, **Cyrillic**, and **Ethiopic**. Writing was also invented independently in other parts of the world, including **Rongorongo** glyphs on Rapa Nui (Easter Island) and **Maya glyphs** in Mesoamerica.

Celts and Germanic peoples

Battersea shield

This richly decorated bronze cover for a Celtic shield may have been thrown into the Thames River in southern Britain as a religious offering.

Early Celtic gold coins from c. 200 BCE were copied from those of Greece and Macedonia.

Celtic coins

This scene from a silver cauldron shows Cernunnos, a Celtic nature god with the antlers of a stag.

Cernunnos

Torcs were twisted bands of gold or silver worn around the neck by wealthy or important Celts.

Snettisham torc

Queen Boudicca of the Iceni, a tribe of Celtic Britons, led an uprising against Roman occupation in 60 CE.

Queen Boudicca

This Celtic helmet from the 4th century BCE has a crest in the form of a bird of prey.

Ciumeşti helmet

A Germanic Vandal goes hunting in this 5th-century Roman-style mosaic from North Africa.

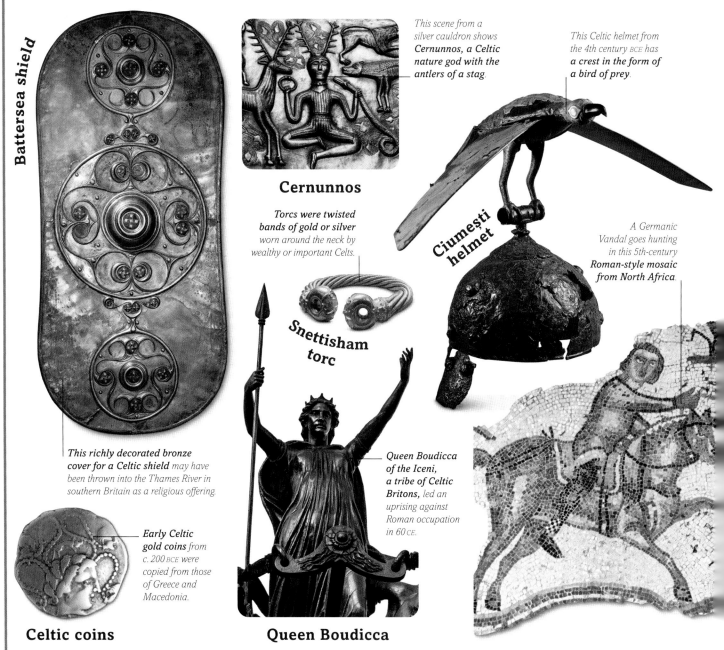

Living to the north of the Roman Empire were Celts in the west and Germanic peoples in the east. Most Celts were conquered and brought into the Roman Empire. In the 5th century CE, the Germanic peoples overran the Western Roman Empire, and founded new Germanic kingdoms.

The Celts had close contact with the Mediterranean world. They issued **Celtic coins** modeled on Greek ones, and adopted the Roman alphabet. Celtic artists made richly patterned metalwork, such as the **Battersea shield** and **Snettisham torc**. They were great warriors, though their armor, such as the

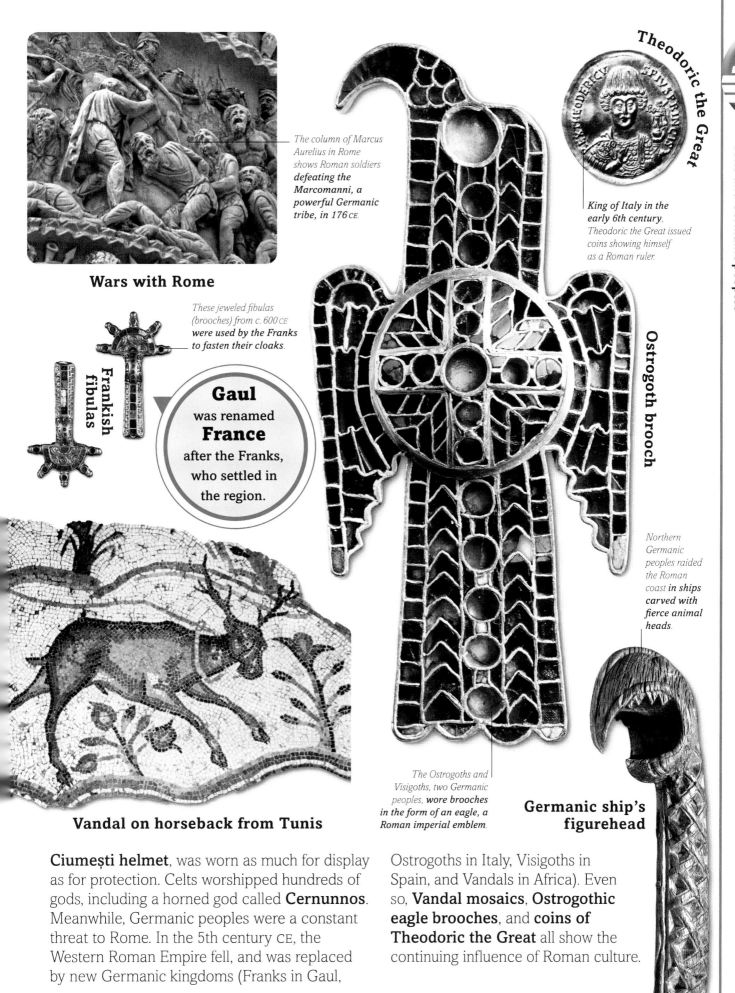

The column of Marcus Aurelius in Rome shows Roman soldiers **defeating the Marcomanni, a powerful Germanic tribe, in 176** CE.

Wars with Rome

These jeweled fibulas (brooches) from c. 600 CE **were used by the Franks to fasten their cloaks.**

Frankish fibulas

Gaul was renamed **France** after the Franks, who settled in the region.

Theodoric the Great

King of Italy in the early 6th century, Theodoric the Great issued coins showing himself as a Roman ruler.

Ostrogoth brooch

Northern Germanic peoples raided the Roman coast **in ships carved with fierce animal heads.**

The Ostrogoths and Visigoths, two Germanic peoples, **wore brooches in the form of an eagle, a Roman imperial emblem.**

Vandal on horseback from Tunis

Germanic ship's figurehead

Ciumești helmet, was worn as much for display as for protection. Celts worshipped hundreds of gods, including a horned god called **Cernunnos**. Meanwhile, Germanic peoples were a constant threat to Rome. In the 5th century CE, the Western Roman Empire fell, and was replaced by new Germanic kingdoms (Franks in Gaul,

Ostrogoths in Italy, Visigoths in Spain, and Vandals in Africa). Even so, **Vandal mosaics, Ostrogothic eagle brooches**, and **coins of Theodoric the Great** all show the continuing influence of Roman culture.

Jewelery

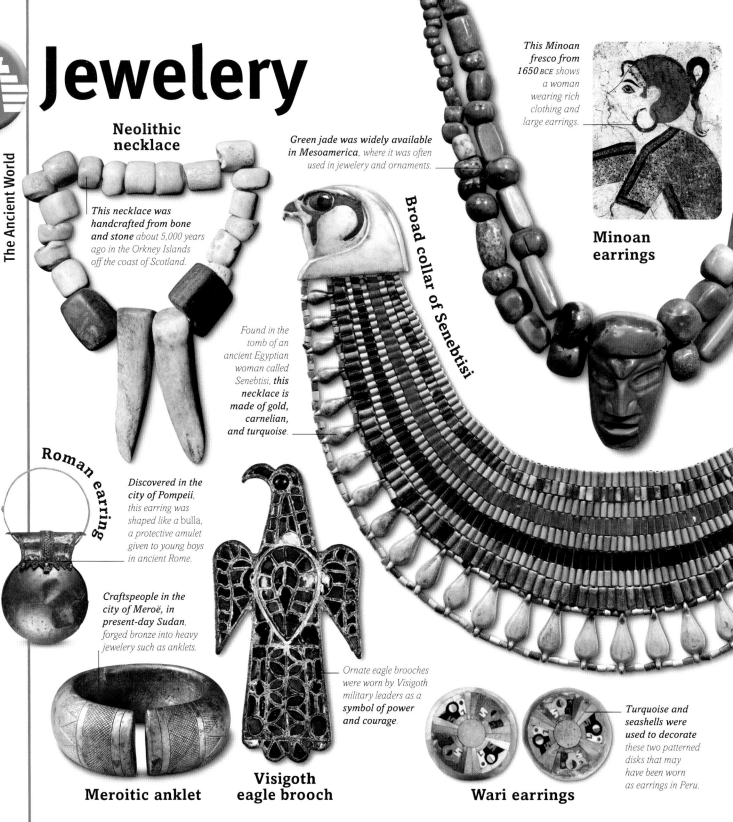

Neolithic necklace

This necklace was handcrafted from bone and stone about 5,000 years ago in the Orkney Islands off the coast of Scotland.

Green jade was widely available in Mesoamerica, where it was often used in jewelery and ornaments.

This Minoan fresco from 1650 BCE shows a woman wearing rich clothing and large earrings.

Minoan earrings

Broad collar of Senebtisi

Found in the tomb of an ancient Egyptian woman called Senebtisi, this necklace is made of gold, carnelian, and turquoise.

Roman earring

Discovered in the city of Pompeii, this earring was shaped like a bulla, a protective amulet given to young boys in ancient Rome.

Craftspeople in the city of Meroë, in present-day Sudan, forged bronze into heavy jewelery such as anklets.

Ornate eagle brooches were worn by Visigoth military leaders as a symbol of power and courage.

Turquoise and seashells were used to decorate these two patterned disks that may have been worn as earrings in Peru.

Meroitic anklet

Visigoth eagle brooch

Wari earrings

Throughout history people have adorned themselves with jewelery. The first forms were basic designs made using natural materials. But over time, master craftspeople honed their skills with precious metals, creating elaborate and expensive pieces. Today, there is more choice than ever before, with the introduction of mass-produced jewelery to suit all tastes and budgets.

With limited materials available, early communities used stones, bones, and teeth to make simple **Neolithic necklaces**. As people developed tools to work with metals, jewelery evolved in different cultures. Ancient Greek and **Roman earrings** were fashioned from gold and worn by rulers and priests to show their high social standing, while many ancient Egyptians wore shiny gold, copper, and glass beads, such as the **broad collar of**

Zapotec jade necklace

The top of this ring is decorated in the shape of a roof, which may symbolize the home of the newly married couple.

Jewish wedding ring

Diamonds, pearls, and enamel adorn this cross, which has symbolized the Christian faith for centuries.

Christian cross

Beautifully bright, beaded headbands and necklaces worn by the Samburu women of Kenya represent their social standing and marital status.

Samburu jewelery

Brass bracelets were made by Yoruba craftspeople in West Africa and given to their leaders and priests to wear during ceremonies.

Yoruba bracelet

The blue feathers of a kingfisher were used to decorate the flowers of this silver hairpin from 19th-century China.

Qing Dynasty hairpin

Materials such as acrylic, glass, and plastic are now used to manufacture cheap but eye-catching costume jewelery.

Costume jewelery

Senebtisi. In Mesoamerica, **jade necklaces** had the highest value. Jewelery also took on symbolic meanings, as seen in **Christian crosses** and **Jewish wedding rings**. Other jewelery remained pretty but practical, such as **Qing Dynasty hairpins** and **Visigoth brooches**. Today, people can also buy **costume jewelery**, which is easier to produce and more affordable.

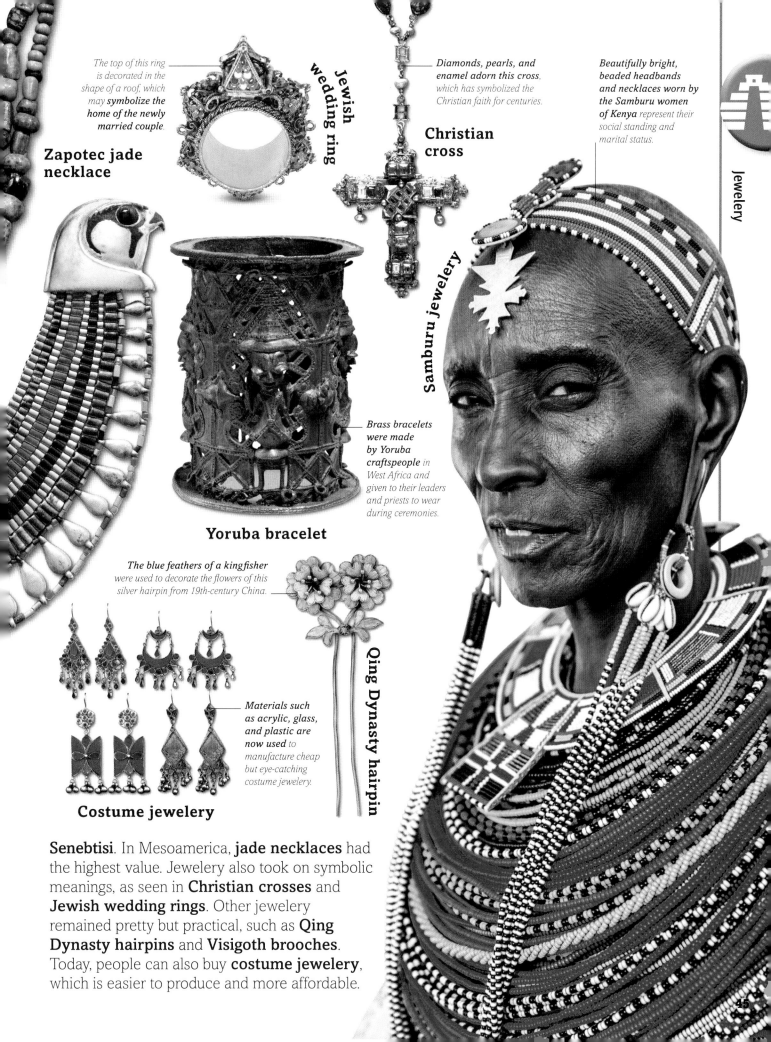

Persian empires

This clay seal describes the conquest of Babylon (in present-day Iraq) by Cyrus the Great.

Cyrus cylinder seal

Darius the Great

Darius standardized gold and silver coins across the empire, stamping them with his own image.

*The archer in this frieze from Darius's palace at Susa may be a **member of the king's personal bodyguard**.*

The Faravahar was an important symbol in the ancient Persian religion of Zoroastrianism, which still has followers today.

Faravahar

*Reached by climbing 111 steps, the Persian capital at Persepolis was **a complex of temples and palaces**.*

*Wealthy and influential Persians displayed their status at royal feasts by **drinking wine from ornately decorated horns**.*

Drinking horn

Frieze of archers from Susa

Persepolis

For more than 1,000 years, the region that is now Iran was ruled by three great Persian empires, one after another. The Persians tolerated other cultures, created elaborate works of art, improved roads and other services, and built a palace whose ruins astonish visitors today.

Cyrus the Great founded the first Persian Empire (also known as the Achaemenid Empire) in 559 BCE. He was a tolerant ruler and allowed conquered peoples to practice their own beliefs, as documented in the **Cyrus cylinder seal**. **Darius the Great** built on Cyrus's legacy, constructing roads and canals, and introducing

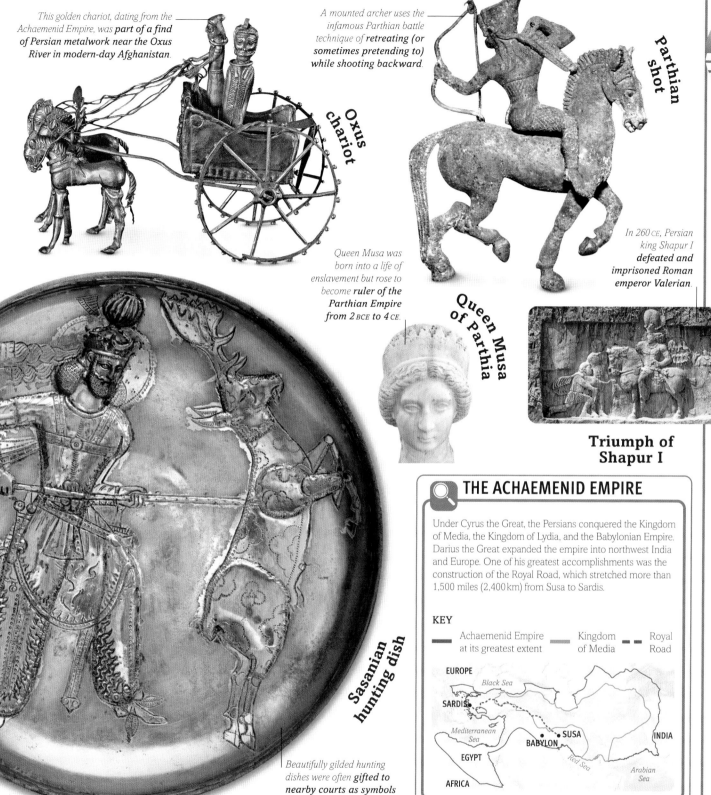

*This golden chariot, dating from the Achaemenid Empire, was **part of a find** of Persian metalwork near the Oxus River in modern-day Afghanistan.*

Oxus chariot

*A mounted archer uses the infamous Parthian battle technique of **retreating** (or sometimes pretending to) while shooting backward.*

Parthian shot

*In 260 CE, Persian king Shapur I **defeated and imprisoned Roman emperor Valerian**.*

*Queen Musa was born into a life of enslavement but rose to become **ruler of the Parthian Empire from 2 BCE to 4 CE**.*

Queen Musa of Parthia

Triumph of Shapur I

Sasanian hunting dish

*Beautifully gilded hunting dishes were often **gifted to nearby courts as symbols of Sasanian power**.*

THE ACHAEMENID EMPIRE

Under Cyrus the Great, the Persians conquered the Kingdom of Media, the Kingdom of Lydia, and the Babylonian Empire. Darius the Great expanded the empire into northwest India and Europe. One of his greatest accomplishments was the construction of the Royal Road, which stretched more than 1,500 miles (2,400 km) from Susa to Sardis.

KEY

— Achaemenid Empire at its greatest extent
— Kingdom of Media
-- Royal Road

EUROPE
Black Sea
SARDIS
Mediterranean Sea
SUSA
BABYLON
EGYPT
Red Sea
INDIA
Arabian Sea
AFRICA

a single currency across the empire. He also began construction of an impressive new capital, **Persepolis**. In 330 BCE, Greek invaders conquered Persia and sacked Persepolis. The region eventually returned to Persian rule in 247 BCE under the Parthian Empire. Skilled warriors, the Parthians were famous for the **Parthian shot**, a battle technique that involved shooting backward from horseback. A third empire, founded by the Sasanian Dynasty in 224 CE, produced wonderful artwork, such as the **Sasanian hunting dish**, and saw its Roman enemy defeated with the **Triumph of Shapur I** in 260 CE.

Mediterranean civilizations

The Phoenicians (c. 1500–300 BCE) were experts in making glass objects, such as this glass-bead pendant.

Phoenician glass-bead

This wall painting was discovered at the palace of Knossos, built by the Minoan civilization (c. 3500–1100 BCE) on the island of Crete.

Minoan bull-leaping fresco

The Phoenicians used mucus taken from a sea snail to make their expensive dye.

Mycenaean gold mask

Tyrian purple dye

Some rulers of the Mycenaean civilization (c. 1600–1100 BCE) were buried with gold masks over their faces.

The ancient city of Carthage (in modern-day Tunisia) became independent from Phoenician dominance around 650 BCE, but later fell to the Romans.

Paestum temple

Ruins of Carthage

Greek colonies spread across the Mediterranean, with new towns and temples being built, such as Paestum in modern-day Italy.

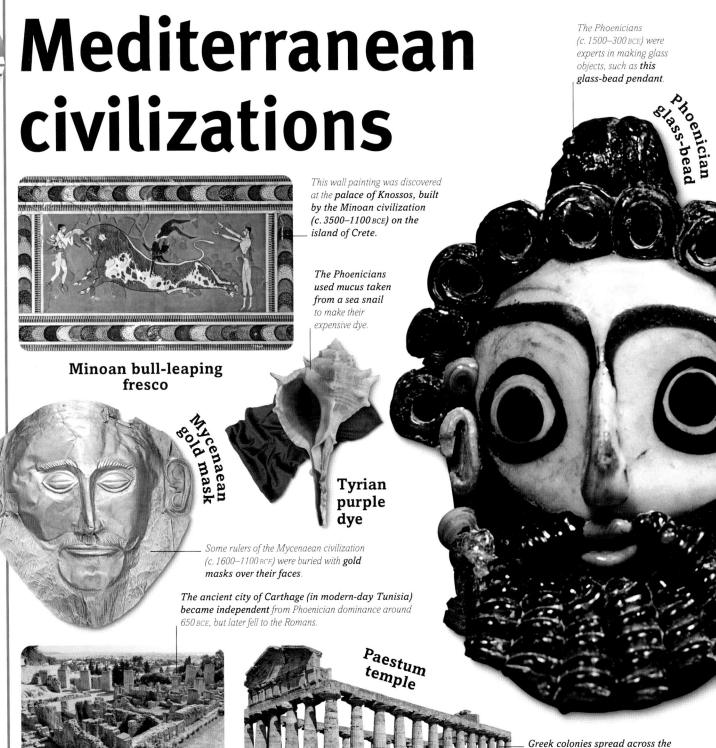

Many ancient civilizations sprang up around the Mediterranean Sea, from the Phoenicians to the Greeks and Etruscans. Interacting with each other over the sea and land, these civilizations not only shared trade routes, but also their cultures and ideas. Many features of modern European cultures can be traced back to these civilizations.

The Minoan civilization flourished on the island of Crete, and left behind striking artwork such as the **bull-leaping fresco**. They were followed by the Mycenaeans of mainland Greece, who built fortified cities and buried their kings with **gold masks**. The Phoenicians were expert sailors and craftspeople who originated along the coast of modern-day Lebanon. They produced and traded

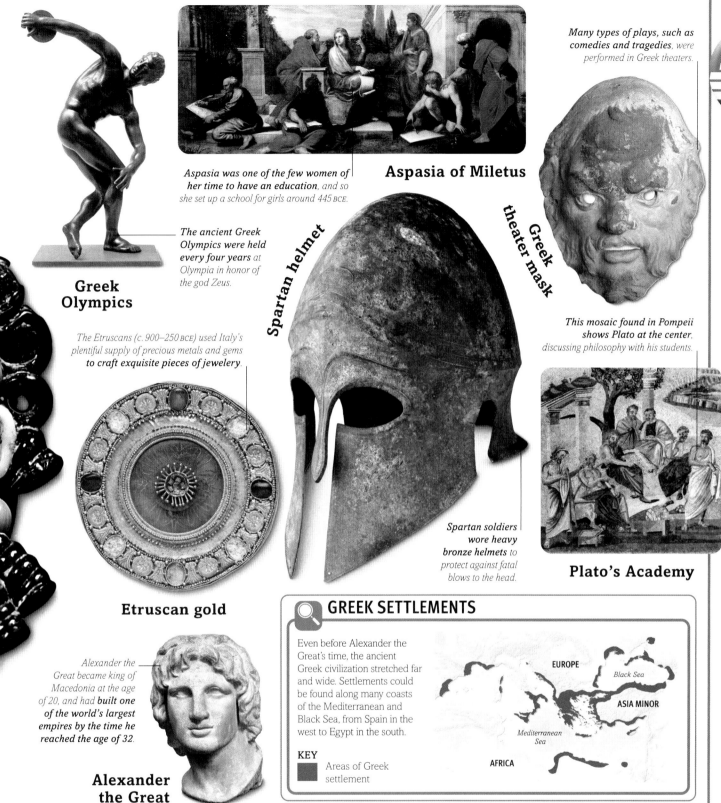

Greek Olympics

The ancient Greek Olympics were held every four years at Olympia in honor of the god Zeus.

Aspasia was one of the few women of her time to have an education, and so she set up a school for girls around 445 BCE.

Aspasia of Miletus

Many types of plays, such as comedies and tragedies, were performed in Greek theaters.

Spartan helmet

Greek theater mask

This mosaic found in Pompeii shows Plato at the center, discussing philosophy with his students.

The Etruscans (c. 900–250 BCE) used Italy's plentiful supply of precious metals and gems to craft exquisite pieces of jewelery.

Etruscan gold

Spartan soldiers wore heavy bronze helmets to protect against fatal blows to the head.

Plato's Academy

Alexander the Great became king of Macedonia at the age of 20, and had built one of the world's largest empires by the time he reached the age of 32.

Alexander the Great

GREEK SETTLEMENTS

Even before Alexander the Great's time, the ancient Greek civilization stretched far and wide. Settlements could be found along many coasts of the Mediterranean and Black Sea, from Spain in the west to Egypt in the south.

EUROPE

Black Sea

ASIA MINOR

Mediterranean Sea

AFRICA

KEY

■ Areas of Greek settlement

Tyrian purple dye, which was so expensive that wearing clothes dyed with it became a symbol of wealth and status. Ancient Greece was a collection of more than 1,000 city-states, such as Sparta and Athens. The Greeks not only created new forms of sculpture, but also new ways of thinking. **Plato's Academy** in Athens became a place to discuss philosophy and new ideas. In 335 BCE, all

of Greece was conquered and united under a Macedonian—**Alexander the Great**. A brilliant tactician, he created an empire stretching from Greece and Egypt to India. Alexander's empire came apart after his death in 323 BCE, and in the 3rd century BCE, a new power, Rome, began to take control of the Mediterranean (see pp.50–51).

The Roman Empire

According to one legend, Rome was founded by the twins Romulus and Remus, who were nursed and raised by a wolf.

Romulus and Remus

This emblem, representing the Roman Senate, was found on Roman currency and official documents.

Agrippina was empress from 49–54 CE, and made many important political decisions, such as making her son, Nero, emperor.

Roman aqueduct

The Pont du Gard aqueduct carried drinking water across the Gard River to what is now the French city of Nîmes.

Roman Senate emblem

Agrippina the Younger

Built in northern England on the orders of Emperor Hadrian, this stone wall stretching 73 miles (118 km) protected the northernmost border of the empire.

*The birthplace of the Roman emperor Septimius Severus, **this site in modern-day Libya was an important city in Roman Africa**.*

Leptis Magna

*This giant amphitheater took nearly a decade to build, and had a **grand opening lasting 100 days, full of games and fighting**.*

Colosseum

Hadrian's Wall

Over a period of 500 years, the small city-state of Rome, founded in the rolling hills of Italy, conquered much of Europe and the lands around the Mediterranean Sea. At its peak, the Roman Empire stretched 2,500 miles (4,000 km) from east to west. It was known for its military might, feats of engineering, and the cultural influence it had on far-off lands.

Rome began as a group of small settlements around the Tiber River c. 753 BCE. By 509 BCE, Rome had become a republic ruled by a group of elected officials called the **Roman Senate**. Roman generals such as **Julius Caesar** expanded the state's territory through successful military campaigns across Europe, western Asia, and North Africa. Rome became an empire under Emperor Augustus in 27 BCE. The ancient Romans were

Roman clothing

Wealthy men wore long robes called togas and women wore sweeping dresses called **pallas,** *while ordinary citizens and enslaved people wore basic tunics.*

People captured and enslaved during wars performed all types of work, including domestic service, but were not paid or given any rights.

Enslaved people

*This terra-cotta horse on wheels may have been **a** **mass-produced, popular toy** for Roman children.*

Children's toy

*This elaborately designed helmet would have been **worn by a gladiator for protection during deadly fights at the Colosseum.***

Gladiator helmet

> The Julian calendar of **365 days** was introduced by Julius Caesar in **45 BCE.**

*Julius Caesar named himself the dictator of Rome and held power **until his assassination by the senators in 44** BCE.*

Roman baths

*The Romans built hundreds of public baths across their empire, which **provided clean, heated water that people used to bathe themselves.***

Julius Caesar

EXTENT OF THE ROMAN EMPIRE

At its greatest extent in 117 CE, the Roman Empire stretched from Britain in the north to the coast of North Africa in the south. At the time, it was split into 51 provinces, each led by its own governor.

BRITAIN

Atlantic Ocean

FRANCE

SPAIN

ITALY GREECE

Black Sea

TURKEY

NORTH AFRICA

Mediterranean Sea

EGYPT

KEY

Roman Empire in 117 CE

extraordinary engineers, constructing road networks to link towns and cities, **aqueducts** to carry fresh water across great distances, communal heated baths, and defensive forts and walls, including **Hadrian's Wall**. The **Colosseum** was opened in 70 CE, and was the site of many bloody gladiator battles. The empire eventually split into two parts, and the Western Roman Empire fell in 476 CE, after repeated attacks from powerful tribes in western Europe.

Indian empires

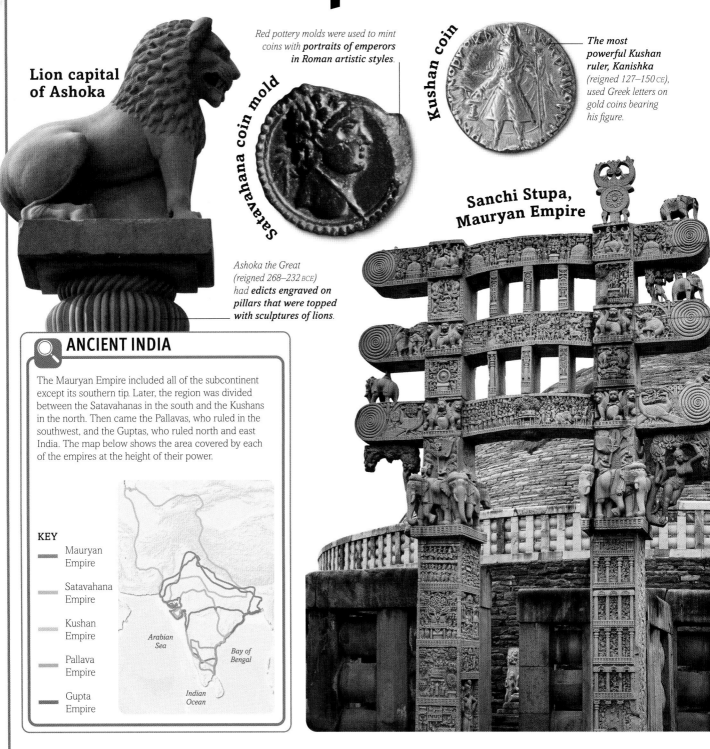

Lion capital of Ashoka

*Red pottery molds were used to mint coins with **portraits of emperors** in Roman artistic styles.*

Satavahana coin mold

Kushan coin

The most powerful Kushan ruler, Kanishka (reigned 127–150 CE), used Greek letters on gold coins bearing his figure.

*Ashoka the Great (reigned 268–232 BCE) had **edicts engraved on pillars that were topped with sculptures of lions**.*

Sanchi Stupa, Mauryan Empire

🔍 ANCIENT INDIA

The Mauryan Empire included all of the subcontinent except its southern tip. Later, the region was divided between the Satavahanas in the south and the Kushans in the north. Then came the Pallavas, who ruled in the southwest, and the Guptas, who ruled north and east India. The map below shows the area covered by each of the empires at the height of their power.

KEY
— Mauryan Empire
— Satavahana Empire
— Kushan Empire
— Pallava Empire
— Gupta Empire

Arabian Sea
Bay of Bengal
Indian Ocean

Between 321 BCE and 900 CE, five great empires rose up in the Indian subcontinent—the Mauryan, Satavahana, Kushan, Pallava, and Gupta empires. The period saw the spread of a new world religion, Buddhism, and the building of the first stone temples for Hindu gods.

The first major Indian empire was established in 321 BCE by Chandragupta Maurya. Although early Mauryans were Hindus, Mauryan emperor Ashoka the Great converted to Buddhism. He built the **Sanchi Stupa** and set up inscribed pillars topped with **lion capitals** across his empire. The Mauryans were succeeded by the

Kushan relief

*Kushan Buddhist reliefs **blended Greek and Indian styles of sculpture**.*

The finest ancient Indian paintings are Buddhist frescoes (wall paintings) made by Gupta artists in the Ajanta Caves of western India.

Gupta astronomer Aryabhata correctly argued that Earth was a rotating sphere.

Aryabhata

Buddhist fresco, Gupta Empire

Mauryan emperor Ashoka built this stupa as a sacred mound to hold relics such as the ashes of the Buddha.

*Gupta temples were decorated with terra-cotta plaques such as this one, which shows the Hindu god **Krishna defeating a horse demon**.*

Krishna carving, Gupta Empire

*The Shore temple, which was built c. 700 CE, is **dedicated to the Hindu gods Shiva and Vishnu**.*

Gupta musical instruments

*This Gupta tile **shows a court musician playing the lute**.*

Shore temple, Pallava Empire

Satavahanas from c. 100 BCE. They traded by sea with the Roman Empire—many **Satavahana coins** were based on Roman coins. Around 30 CE, a northern empire was founded by the Kushans, who were Buddhists from Central Asia. Many sculptors in their empire carved Buddhist **reliefs**. The Pallavas (275–897 CE) and Guptas (320–554 CE) were Hindus, but also supported Buddhism. They built richly decorated Hindu temples, such as the Pallava **Shore temple**. The Gupta period is now seen as India's Golden Age. Buddhist art flourished and scientists, such as **Aryabhata**, made new discoveries.

The ancient Americas

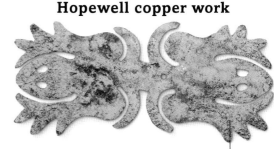

The people of the Hopewell culture believed copper was sacred and traveled far to get it.

Almost 1,300 ft (411 m) long, the Serpent Mound still snakes across Adams County in Ohio.

Hopewell smoking pipe

This beaver-shaped pipe was used by people of the Hopewell culture (c. 200 BCE–500 CE) during prayers and celebrations.

Serpent Mound

Mercury in the soil has dirtied the jade of this Maya artwork, but it was once a brilliantly glowing green.

The Maya (c. 1800 BCE–1697 CE) used pottery to create vessels for everyday use as well as for ritual purposes.

Maya pottery

Jade figurine

The Maya blew air through the vessel's spout into a liquid chocolate mixture to create a frothy top over the drink's surface.

Olmec sculpture

The Olmec people (c. 1200–400 BCE) of Mesoamerica sculpted giant heads, some up to 9 ft (3 m) tall, which are thought to be portraits of their rulers.

The Aztecs (c. 1345–1521) gave the abandoned city of Teotihuacán its name, which means "city of the gods."

Teotihuacán

Chocolate vessel

The first great civilization to emerge in the Americas was that of the Norte Chico in modern-day Peru. It was one of the oldest and most sophisticated civilizations of the ancient world. Later, larger ancient civilizations developed in South and Central America, and southern North America.

The first known city in the Americas was built by the Norte Chico people around 3000 BCE. They took on Peru's challenging deserts to construct what are now called the **Caral ruins**. Peru is also home to the remnants of other ancient civilizations, such as the **Nazca lines** and **Moche ceramics**. In the Maya cities of Mesoamerica, cocoa beans were

Zapotec urn

Ceramic burial urns were used to store the remains of important people in the Zapotec civilization (700 BCE–1521 CE).

The Caral ruins cover an area of 2.5 sq miles (6.26 sq km), and **contain six massive pyramids**.

Caral ruins

The ceramic jars of the Moche people (c. 100–700 CE) had unusual handles that might have been shaped to stop water from evaporating in Peru's hot climate.

Peru's Chavín civilization (c. 900–200 BCE) considered the **puma to be a symbol of Earth's power**.

Chavín puma relief sculpture

Moche ceramics

The Nazca (c. 200 BCE–600 CE) covered the Peruvian desert with **large-scale drawings of shapes, spirals, and animals**.

The Paracas people (900 BCE–400 CE) wrapped their dead in richly colored embroidered textiles, which retain their color even today.

Paracas **textiles** required long periods of work and a lot of resources to make.

Paracas textiles

Nazca lines

farmed and then mixed with other ingredients in specialized **chocolate vessels** to make a frothy drink. Mesoamerica is also the site of the legendary city **Teotihuacán**, although no one is quite sure who built it. In North America, Indigenous cultures such as the Adena and Fort Ancient peoples molded hills to create huge effigies (sculpted figures) in the shape of animals—the biggest of which is the **Serpent Mound**. It is thought to have been used for religious ceremonies. Effigies from the Hopewell culture often came in smaller sizes, such as the beaver-shaped **smoking pipe**, or frog-shaped **copper work**.

Ancient Africa

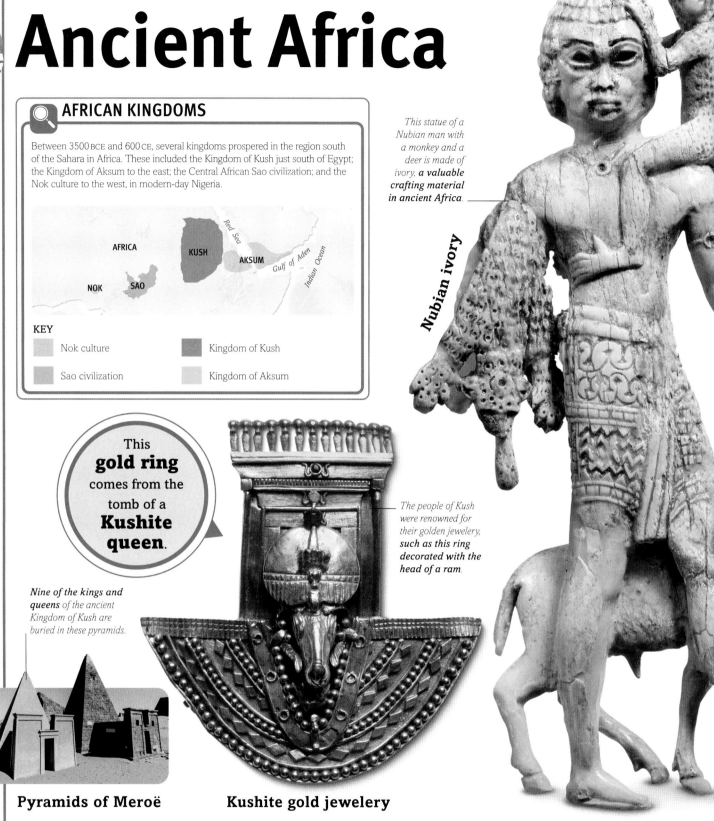

*This statue of a Nubian man with a monkey and a deer is made of ivory, **a valuable crafting material in ancient Africa**.*

Nubian ivory

This **gold ring** comes from the tomb of a **Kushite queen**.

*The people of Kush were renowned for their golden jewelry, **such as this ring decorated with the head of a ram**.*

*Nine of the kings and **queens** of the ancient Kingdom of Kush are buried in these pyramids.*

Pyramids of Meroë

Kushite gold jewelery

While North Africa was home to one of the earliest civilizations in the world, ancient Egypt, many civilizations south of the Sahara, such as Aksum, Kush, Nok, and Sao, also flourished. **They constructed impressive temples and monuments, and left behind stunning jewelry and pottery.**

The Kingdom of Kush (in present-day Sudan) flourished from c. 1000 BCE until c. 350 CE. The **pyramids of Meroë** were the resting place of the kingdom's kings and queens. A Kushite queen was known as a kandake, and kandakes often wore elaborate **gold jewelry** or owned sculptures made of **ivory**. In the 4th century CE,

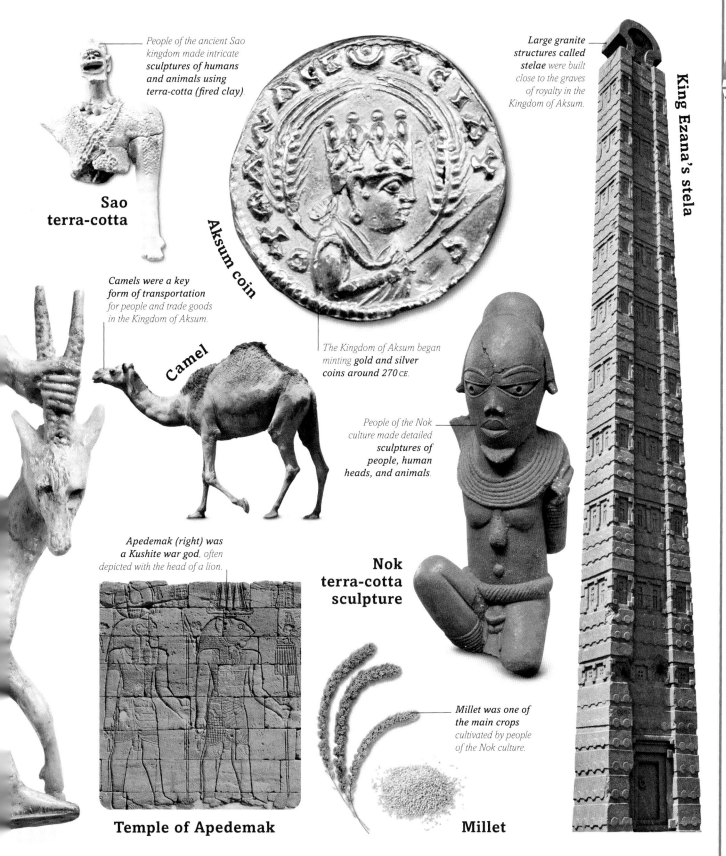

People of the ancient Sao kingdom made intricate **sculptures of humans and animals** using terra-cotta (fired clay).

Sao terra-cotta

Camels were a key form of transportation for people and trade goods in the Kingdom of Aksum.

Camel

Aksum coin

Large granite structures called **stelae** *were built close to the graves of royalty in the Kingdom of Aksum.*

King Ezana's stela

The Kingdom of Aksum began minting **gold and silver coins** around 270 CE.

People of the Nok culture made detailed **sculptures of people, human heads, and animals**.

Nok terra-cotta sculpture

Apedemak (right) was a Kushite war god, often depicted with the head of a lion.

Temple of Apedemak

Millet was one of the main crops cultivated by people of the Nok culture.

Millet

the kingdom fell into decline, and was invaded by the Kingdom of Aksum (in present-day Ethiopia and Eritrea). Aksum was another wealthy kingdom, which grew rich through trade. It minted its own **gold coins** and constructed elaborate granite towers known as **stelae**. In Central Africa, from the 4th century BCE, the Sao civilization became known for its **terra-cotta pottery** and metalwork. At the same time, farther west in present-day Nigeria, the Nok culture was farming **millet** and creating incredibly detailed **terra-cotta sculptures** of human heads and animals.

THE MEDIEVAL WORLD

The Medieval World

The thousand years between the late 5th and 15th centuries saw Christianity and Islam spread out across Eurasia and Africa, with China, India, and Africa south of the Sahara also experiencing a golden age of culture and prosperity.

In Europe, Western historians have traditionally known the period between the end of the ancient world and start of modern times as the "Middle Ages." This era begins (in Europe, at least) sometime around the fall of Rome in 476 CE and ends with the beginning of the Renaissance and the Scientific Revolution in the 15th and 16th centuries. Outside Europe, though, there was not always a clear break between the ancient world and the medieval period.

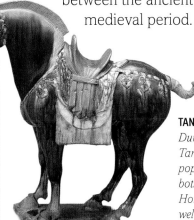

TANG HORSE SCULPTURE
During the golden age of the Tang Dynasty, horses were popular subjects in art, in both sculptures and paintings. Horses symbolized wealth, as well as China's expansion into new lands.

East Asian empires

In China, the Han Dynasty had collapsed by the early 3rd century CE, but the empire was reunified in the 6th century. The Tang came to power in the early 7th century and the Song in the 10th century. Under these dynasties, China experienced a golden age of prosperity, as well as artistic achievement and technological innovation.

To the east of China, Korea was unified in the 7th century under the Silla. A series of dynasties followed, with the Joseon Dynasty ruling Korea

from the 14th to the late 19th centuries. By contrast, though imperial Japan experienced a cultural golden age from the 9th century, by the end of the 12th century the power of the emperor had weakened, and Japan came under the control of warlords known as shoguns.

Maritime traders and explorers

To the south of China, the Chola Dynasty of southern India extended its influence into the islands of Southeast Asia, reaching its height between the 9th and 13th centuries. Around the same time, a number of kingdoms sprang up in mainland Southeast Asia, on trade routes running between India and China. These kingdoms, such as Angkor in Cambodia and Pagan in Burma, were heavily influenced by the religions of Hinduism and Buddhism.

The Lapita people of Southeast Asia had begun to explore the Pacific from as early as 3000 BCE, and by around 200 CE, most of its islands had been discovered. Over the next thousand years the remaining islands—such as Hawaii in the north, Rapa Nui (Easter Island) in the east, and New Zealand in the south—were settled.

American cultures

Cultures in the Americas flourished throughout the medieval period. In Mesoamerica, the Maya civilization continued to thrive until around 950 CE, when conflict and drought probably caused their empire to crumble. Toward the end of the era, the Aztecs and Inca created powerful empires in modern-day Mexico and the Andes mountains of South America respectively.

In North America, the varied environments across the continent led to many distinct cultural groups, from the Dorset people of the frozen Arctic to the Hohokam of the dry, hot regions in what is now Arizona. One of the largest pre-Columbian North American civilizations, that of the Mississippian culture, thrived in the fertile valleys of the Mississippi River.

The wealth of Africa

Though ancient Egyptian civilization declined after Egypt was invaded by—and became part of—the Roman Empire, the abundance of natural resources on the continent led to the growth of African civilizations further south during the medieval era. Many kingdoms south of the Sahara, such as the Kingdom of Zimbabwe, the Kilwa Sultanate, and the Mali Empire, flourished and became wealthy in this period through trade in salt, gold, and other sought-after goods. These civilizations used their wealth to build great cities, each having its own unique architectural styles.

GREAT ZIMBABWE VASE
Pottery and other artifacts found at the ruined medieval settlement of Great Zimbabwe suggest that it was once a bustling trading center.

CHATEAU GAILLARD
The ruins of this 12th-century castle in Normandy, France, display many features of early medieval castle design. The main keep sits high on a hill, surrounded by three walled enclosures and dry moats.

A new religion

As Christianity continued to spread across much of Europe, a new religion, Islam, emerged in the Arabian Peninsula. A series of Islamic empires quickly spread the new faith across the Middle East and into North Africa. Islamic culture saw a golden age between the 8th and 13th centuries, but this period also saw clashes over holy sites with the Christian kingdoms of Europe, who invaded Muslim territory in a series of crusades.

North American cultures

The Dorset people were highly skilled in craftwork, using wood or animal bones to create striking objects.

Carved antler, Dorset culture

The Thule people used whale rib bones as frames for their homes.

Whale-rib home

Umiaks, or Thule whaling boats (shown in this model), were made from animal skin, wood, and flexible whalebone (baleen).

The handle of this drum, carved in the shape of a whale, indicates the Thule people's deep connection with the animals they hunted.

Thule drum

Umiak

The Mogollon culture (c. 200–1450 CE) may have been the first to make pottery in the American Southwest.

These delicate bracelets are made of the shells of the glycymeris clam.

The Hohokam's ceremonial ball games may have been influenced by similar games from Mesoamerica.

Mogollon pottery

Hohokam ball court

Hohokam shell bracelets

Indigenous cultures of North America ranged from nomadic peoples who lived in the freezing northern regions to societies that settled and built vast cities in the southwestern deserts and in river valleys. These cultures were often distinct, partly due to the varied environments of the continent. People worked with their surroundings, using what was available to their advantage.

The **Dorset people** (c. 800 BCE–1300 CE) lived in the harsh environment of Arctic North America. They inhabited areas close to the shore, living in animal-skin tents and moving from place to place when the seasons changed. They were succeeded by the Thule people (c. 1000 CE onward) who built permanent settlements that included **whale-rib homes**. The Hohokam (c. 200–1450 CE) lived further south, in dry areas

The Makah people carved images of whales and people into rocks close to their home in Ozette (near present-day Neah Bay in Washington).

Makah petroglyphs

*This Ancestral Puebloan construction in Mesa Verde National Park, CO, is the **largest of the region's cliff dwellings**, with around 150 rooms.*

Cliff Palace, Mesa Verde

Ancestral Puebloan ceramics were colored using white clay and black paint, which was often obtained by boiling plants.

Ancestral Puebloans

The **rattle** in the frog's hand is similar to those used in religious ceremonies.

Makah artifacts, such as this mask, were preserved in excellent condition after a mudslide buried a Makah settlement in Ozette, WA.

Makah mask

This frog-shaped pipe was found at the ancient city of Cahokia—the largest urban settlement of the Mississippian cultures.

Mississippian pipe

*The Mandan people settled along the Missouri River and **built homes in the earth** that had turf roofs.*

Mandan earth lodge

of what is now Arizona. They grew maize and lived in towns that had **ball courts** for ceremonial purposes. The **Ancestral Puebloans** (c. 100–1600 CE) were undaunted by Colorado's rocky terrain and set about building multi-story structures, including the **Cliff Palace at Mesa Verde**. In the fertile valleys of the Mississippi River, **Mississippian cultures** (c. 700–1600 CE) thrived, with artists and craftspeople creating new designs and sculpture.

The spread of Islam

The oldest mosque in Africa, the Great Mosque in Tunisia was first constructed in 670 CE and rebuilt in 836 CE.

Great Mosque of Kairouan

This great library housed many rare books, and scholars were invited to translate books into Arabic to add to the collection.

House of Wisdom

Fatimid pendant

The Egypt-based Fatimid Empire (909–1171 CE) controlled gold mines, and used the precious metal they provided to make valuable jewelery.

Built by the Umayyad Caliphate (661–750 CE), the Dome of the Rock is one of Islam's holiest sites.

Dome of the Rock

🔍 ISLAMIC KINGDOMS

In just more than 100 years, Islamic kingdoms spread their rule from the Arabian Peninsula to parts of North Africa, Spain, and Central and South Asia. This was achieved through a mixture of conquest, trade, and religious conversion.

KEY

▪ Spread by 632 CE
▪ Spread by 656 CE
▪ Spread by 756 CE

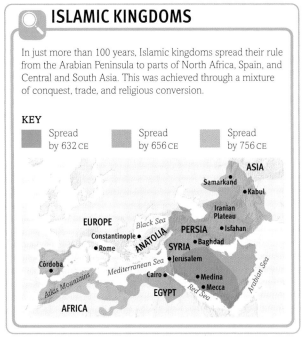

ASIA
Samarkand
Kabul
Iranian Plateau
EUROPE
Black Sea
Constantinople
ANATOLIA
PERSIA
Isfahan
Rome
SYRIA
Baghdad
Córdoba
Mediterranean Sea
Jerusalem
Arabian Sea
Atlas Mountains
Cairo
Medina
Red Sea
Mecca
EGYPT
AFRICA

After the death of the Prophet Muhammad in 632 CE, a series of empires expanded Islamic rule and influence. The greatest of these was ruled by the Abbasid Dynasty of Baghdad (750–1258 CE), who presided over a Golden Age of Islam that saw great progress in medicine, mathematics, and astronomy.

Knowledge was highly prized during this time and large libraries were built all over the Islamic world. In Baghdad, the caliph (ruler) **Harun Al-Rashid** had books from other languages translated into Arabic and kept in the **House of Wisdom**. Muslim scientists and scholars wrote many books, one of the most important being *The Canon of*

Harun Al-Rashid

A real ruler, Caliph Harun Al-Rashid (reigned 786–809 CE) was made into a lead character in the stories of The Thousand and One Nights.

Seljuk glazed tiles

The Seljuks of Anatolia (in present-day Turkey) were known for their ceramic blue tiles, which they used to decorate buildings.

The Canon of Medicine

Written in 1025 CE, Ibn Sina's work listed contagious diseases and explained how dirty water causes infection.

Geometric designs

Patterns of circles, squares, multi-sided polygons, and stars were popular designs in Islamic art and decoration.

An astrolabe was a handheld model of the universe used by Islamic astronomers to study the planets and stars.

Fatimid astrolabe

The Moroccan Marinid Dynasty (1244–1465 CE) decorated their buildings with wooden panels that were intricately carved with shapes and Arabic words.

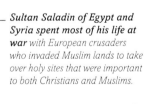

Marinid carving

Mamluk glassware

Sultan Saladin of Egypt and Syria spent most of his life at war with European crusaders who invaded Muslim lands to take over holy sites that were important to both Christians and Muslims.

The Mamluks of Egypt (1250–1517) made beautiful glassware by coating its surface with gold or enamel (powdered glass).

Sultan Saladin

This tower was built by Qutub-ud-Din Aibak, the first Muslim ruler of Delhi.

Qutub Minar

Medicine. Written by Ibn Sina, it was translated and used as a medical textbook for 600 years in Europe. As knowledge spread across the Islamic world, so, too, did Islamic styles of architecture, each style evolving to use a region's unique materials. In Tunisia, the **Great Mosque of Kairouan** was constructed from mud bricks. In Delhi, India, the establishment of Islamic rule was marked by the construction of a tall sandstone tower, the **Qutub Minar**. In Jerusalem, the **Dome of the Rock** showed off geometric patterns with its blue-glazed tiles.

Europe awakens

*This bust contains the skull of Charlemagne, who united the small kingdoms of western Europe **and became the Holy Roman Emperor**.*

Charlemagne

The Byzantine Empire produced exquisite religious art, *such as this mosaic showing Jesus Christ.*

Christ Pantocrator mosaic

*The crown belonging to Recceswinth, 7th-century king of the Visigoths in Spain, **shows the skill and craftsmanship of this Germanic people**.*

*Banished from Iceland, Erik the Red **set up a settlement on Greenland in the 10th century**.*

Visigoth votive crown

*Byzantine emperor Justinian tried to restore the Roman Empire to its former glory, **conquering much of Italy and North Africa**.*

Justinian I

*Built in 412 CE, the defensive walls of Constantinople **provided the city with protection for much of the next millennium**.*

Theodosian Walls

Following the capture of Rome by barbarian tribes, most of western Europe came under the rule of a series of smaller Germanic kingdoms. To the east, however, the former Roman Empire flourished in the form of the Byzantine Empire, while further north a new power was emerging in Kyiv.

The last emperor of Rome was deposed by a Germanic general, Odoacer, in 476 CE. Just 17 years later, however, Odoacer was ousted by Theodoric, King of the Ostrogoths. Theodoric respected Roman culture; his **Mausoleum** in Ravenna showed his appreciation for Roman architecture. Farther east, the Byzantine Empire

The Ostrogoths, a Germanic tribe that settled in Italy, buried their dead wearing exquisite jewelery.

Ostrogothic belt buckle

The daughter of Alfred the Great, Æthelflæd ruled the English kingdom of Mercia and led her armies against the Danes.

Æthelflæd

The most powerful of the Germanic kings, Theodoric the Great was buried in Ravenna.

Mausoleum of Theodoric

Viking longships had a **single sail** and up to **60 rowers**.

Helmets made from steel plates, chain mail, and fur-lined cheek flaps **protected the warrior's head and neck.**

King of Wessex in southwest England, Alfred defeated the Vikings, who controlled much of Britain.

Alfred the Great

Viking helmet

Erik the Red

Viking women and men wore beautifully crafted brooches to fasten their clothing.

A Viking warrior, Oleg seized Kyiv in 882, establishing what later became the powerful Kievan Rus state.

Canute became king of England in 1016, of Denmark in 1018, and of Norway in 1028.

Oleg of Novgorod

Viking brooch

King Canute

prospered, expanding greatly under **Justinian I**, and creating fine artwork such as the **Christ Pantocrator mosaic**. In the late 8th century, the Frankish king **Charlemagne** united much of western and central Europe, and in 800 declared himself the first Holy Roman Emperor. To the north, the Vikings of Scandinavia raided in their longships, and settled in Britain, Ireland, Iceland, and Greenland. In eastern Europe, the Viking prince **Oleg of Novgorod** took control of Kyiv. This laid the foundations for Kievan Rus, a state that the modern nations of Ukraine, Belarus, and Russia all claim as a cultural ancestor.

Medieval Europe

Imperial Crown of the Holy Roman Empire

The Imperial Crown is decorated with **144 precious stones**.

*The crown was used in the coronations of all the Holy Roman Emperors **from the 10th century until 1806**.*

*During the rule of **Boris I**, Bulgaria expanded its territory, and the Bulgarians converted to Christianity.*

Boris I of Bulgaria

*This 12th-century casket decorated with images of Jesus Christ and the saints **was used to store small sacred objects**.*

The Bayeux Tapestry

Showing the Norman conquest of England in 1066, the Bayeux Tapestry is more than 230 ft (70 m) long.

*The First Crusade resulted in **Christian soldiers capturing Jerusalem from the Muslim Fatimid Caliphate**.*

The First Crusade

At the height of the medieval era, Europe was dominated by powerful kings who exchanged land with nobles for loyalty. But most people were peasants working on land owned by lords. Most of Europe was Christian, and the Catholic Church called for Crusades to conquer the Holy Land in the Middle East.

The strongest European state in this period was the Holy Roman Empire, with the **Imperial Crown** providing a striking symbol of its power. Emperor **Frederick Barbarossa**, who ruled in the 12th century, was one of the empire's most charismatic leaders, consolidating his power over most of Germany. In France, King **Philip II**

Frederick Barbarossa

This golden bust shows Frederick Barbarossa, one of the **greatest of the Holy Roman Emperors**.

King Philip II

The first ruler to call himself King of France, Philip II turned his country into the most powerful in Europe.

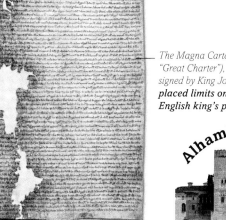

Magna Carta

The Magna Carta (or "Great Charter"), signed by King John, **placed limits on the English king's power**.

Alhambra

*The palace and fortress was built by the **Muslim rulers of Granada** in southern Spain.*

*Between 1347 and 1351, about 25 million Europeans died of **a plague that was carried by fleas living on rats**.*

The Black Death

*France and England fought for more than 100 years **over claims to the French throne**.*

The Hundred Years' War

*Serbian king Stefan Dušan issued a **collection of laws** in the 14th century, which covered all aspects of life.*

Dušan's Code

Christian symbols

maintained absolute power over his nobles. But in England, King John was forced by his barons to sign the **Magna Carta** in 1215, which limited the power of the king. In Serbia, **Dušan's Code** was written during the rule of King Stefan Dušan, providing the Serbian people with an agreed set of laws. Wars were common, with the longest lasting for 116 years. The Pope held absolute power as head of the Church, and in 1095, the **First Crusade** began when Christian armies traveled to Jerusalem to claim the city from its Muslim rulers. It was the first of many such crusades over the following two centuries.

The Mongol Empire

Genghis Khan

*Temüjin, a skilled military commander, united the Mongol tribes and **was declared Genghis Khan ("Universal Ruler") in 1206**.*

The Golden Horde

Batu Khan established the Golden Horde, a state that would come to include Russia, Hungary, and other parts of eastern Europe, in 1227.

The siege of Baghdad

The Mongol army sacked Baghdad in 1258, bringing the Islamic Abbasid Empire to an end.

Mongol iron helmets had a fur trim *to keep the warrior's head warm in the windy, cold lands.*

Kublai Khan

A grandson of Genghis Khan, Kublai completed his grandfather's conquest of China, where he established the Yuan Dynasty in 1271.

Warrior's helmet

The Mongol Empire was founded by the nomadic warrior Genghis Khan in 1206. His army was feared for its speed and aggression, and over the next 20 years it conquered northern China and much of Central Asia. The Mongols went on to build the largest land empire the world had ever seen.

Following the death of **Genghis Khan** in 1227, his grandsons **Batu Khan** and **Kublai Khan** extended the empire into eastern Europe and the rest of China. Their armies were often brutal: cities that refused to surrender were destroyed. One example was **Baghdad**, the capital of the Abbasid Caliphate, which was sacked in 1258.

This metal tablet was a kind of travel document that assured the traveler protection and free passage on the Silk Road.

Paiza

EXTENT OF THE MONGOL EMPIRE

At its greatest extent, in 1279, the Mongol Empire covered much of Asia and eastern Europe, including Yuan China, Persia (present-day Iran), and the steppe heartlands. The Mongols ruled their empire from the center but relied on the foreigners they employed to manage day-to-day affairs.

EUROPE

YUAN DYNASTY

ASIA

Khanbaliq (Beijing)

Samarkand

KEY

Baghdad

Balkh

Luoyang

Iranian Plateau

CHINA

Mongol Empire at its height

Major Silk Road routes

Himalayas

ARABIA

INDIA

The Mongols were expert horse riders, who could travel up to 80 miles (130 km) a day across mountains and desert.

Merchants, diplomats, and messengers traveled on the Silk Road, the network of trade routes kept safe by Mongol troops.

Mongol horse riders

The Silk Road

White porcelain decorated with blue glaze originated in western Asia, and became popular in China during the Yuan Dynasty.

Genghis Khan's great-great-granddaughter Khutulun was a **skilled warrior and wrestler who is said to have never lost a fight.**

Khutulun

Yuan pottery

Timur

Timur dreamed of rebuilding Genghis Khan's empire—during his reign (1370–1405), he conquered much of western Asia.

The Mongol army's success can be credited to the riding and archery skills of their **horse riders**. As the empire grew, the Mongols took control of the **Silk Road**, a network of trading routes across Asia. To ensure safety on these routes, the Mongols introduced the **paiza**, an early form of passport that guaranteed protection. In the late 14th century, another great Mongol leader, **Timur**, expanded the empire into India, Persia, and parts of Turkey.

Medieval African kingdoms

Moses Georgios was king of Makuria, one of three kingdoms in medieval Nubia (a region in present-day Sudan and Egypt).

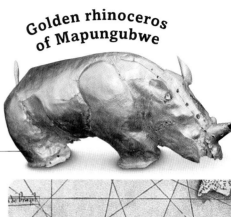

This gold rhinoceros was found in a royal grave in Mapungubwe, one of the first kingdoms in southern Africa.

King Moses Georgios of Makuria

Bird sculptures carved from soft soapstone rock were placed on top of columns in the city of Great Zimbabwe in southern Africa.

Soapstone sculpture from Great Zimbabwe

Mansa Musa

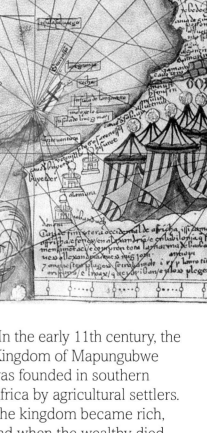

*Mansa Musa, the 14th-century king of the Mali Empire, was famous for his immense wealth and is **shown in this medieval map holding a gold nugget and a golden scepter**.*

AFRICAN KINGDOMS

The medieval era saw a number of kingdoms flourish in Africa. These included the Ghana Empire and Mali Empire in West Africa, the Zagwe Dynasty and Kilwa Sultanate in East Africa, and the Kingdom of Great Zimbabwe in southern Africa.

KEY

- Ghana Empire
- Kilwa Sultanate
- Great Zimbabwe
- Zagwe Kingdom
- Mali Empire

GHANA EMPIRE
MALI • Timbuktu
Jenne
Red Sea
ZAGWE KINGDOM
KILWA SULTANATE
• Mogadishu
Indian Ocean
Atlantic Ocean
GREAT ZIMBABWE
Kalahari Desert

This bronze sculpture comes from Ife, a town in present-day Nigeria that was an important center for religion, culture, and trade.

Ife sculpture

Between 600 and 1450, many great kingdoms and empires flourished across Africa. The African continent was rich in natural resources, such as gold and salt, and many kingdoms became important trading centers and prospered. The wealth generated from trade was used to build large cities, which displayed each kingdom's unique architecture.

In the early 11th century, the Kingdom of Mapungubwe was founded in southern Africa by agricultural settlers. The kingdom became rich, and when the wealthy died, they were buried with beautiful gold artifacts, such as the

*In West Africa, the Kingdom of Nri, founded by the Igbo people in the 10th century, **produced sophisticated bronze sculptures**.*

Igbo bronze vessel

Djenné Mosque

*The world's largest **mud-brick building**, the Djenné Mosque of Mali, was originally constructed in the medieval era but was rebuilt in 1907.*

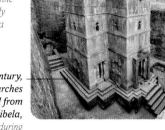

In the 13th century, 11 Christian churches were carved from solid rock in Lalibela, Ethiopia, during the reign of Emperor Gebre Meskel.

Zagwe Dynasty rock-hewn church

*African, Asian, Arab, Persian, and European traders came to this thriving port in East Africa to **sell gold, silver, and pearls**.*

Kilwa Kisiwani

*Kilwa Kisiwani controlled much of the coast of East Africa and started **minting its own coins in the 11th century**.*

Kilwa coins

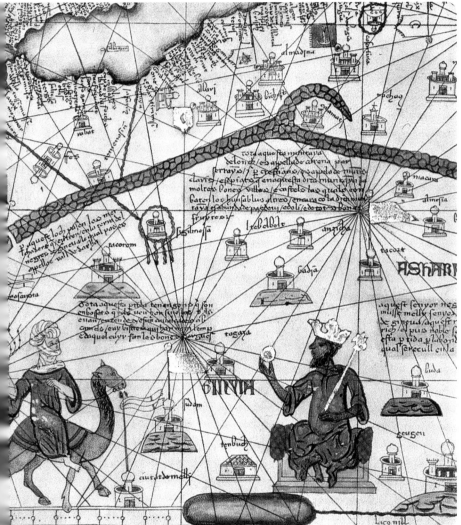

famous **golden rhinoceros**. To the north of Mapungubwe was the Kingdom of Zimbabwe, founded by the Shona people in the 11th century. Zimbabwe, in the Shona language, means "stone houses." Among the few artifacts left from Great Zimbabwe today are **soapstone bird sculptures**. In East Africa, the Kilwa Sultanate expanded steadily from the 11th century as foreign trade flourished. **Kilwa coins** found as far away as Australia may be evidence of the long routes over which its merchants traded goods. In 14th-century West Africa, the Mali Empire became rich through trade in gold and salt, and was ruled by one of the wealthiest people on Earth, **Mansa Musa**.

GREAT ZIMBABWE
From the 11th to the 15th centuries, Great Zimbabwe was the capital of a flourishing Shona state in southern Africa. A key structure of this ancient settlement that remains today is the Great Enclosure seen above, which may have held the royal palace. Its massive walls, some as high as 33 ft (11 m), were built using stone from the surrounding hills.

Great Zimbabwe was established by the ancestors of the Shona people of southern Africa. Ancient Shona states were great trading centers, and controlled the gold trade between inland regions and the Indian Ocean. Great Zimbabwe was largely abandoned by the 15th century, but many *daga* (earthen and mud-brick) buildings as well as granite walls survive today. Its Great Enclosure also contains some smaller structures that may have once been used as community areas, living quarters, or places for artisans to work and sell their goods. Archaeologists have found elaborate stone carvings, gold jewelery, and pottery among its ruins.

Medieval Korea

Silla royal crowns were shaped like tree branches, and were worn only during ceremonial rites.

*Seon-deok was the first of three queens to rule the Silla kingdom, and **was the first female ruler of medieval Korea.***

Queen Seon-deok of Silla

During the Silla period, wealthy people placed tiles with glaring faces on the roofs of houses to scare off evil spirits.

Silla roof tile

Silla gold crown

The oldest surviving observatory in Asia, Cheomseongdae (the tower of the moon and stars) was built in 634 CE.

A geobukseon warship (turtle ship) had a protective roof with metal spikes that could withstand enemy attacks.

Cheomseongdae observatory

General Kim Yu-Shin believed that the Korean peninsula should be united under Silla rule.

Goryeo artisans created ceramics that had a distinct gray-green glaze, which came to be known as celadon or "green-ware."

General Kim Yu-Shin

Goryeo celadon pottery

Until the 7th century CE, three rival kingdoms ruled different parts of the Korean peninsula—the Silla, Baekje, and Goguryeo. The Silla eventually took over the peninsula to form one kingdom. They were followed by the Goryeo, and then the Joseon Dynasty.

During the period of the three kingdoms, the Silla built a large capital and buried their kings in elaborate tombs with treasures such as **gold crowns**. Silla queen **Seon-deok**, a keen astronomer, ordered the **Cheomseongdae observatory** to be built. In 668, under **General Kim Yu-Shin**, the Silla took over the Baekje

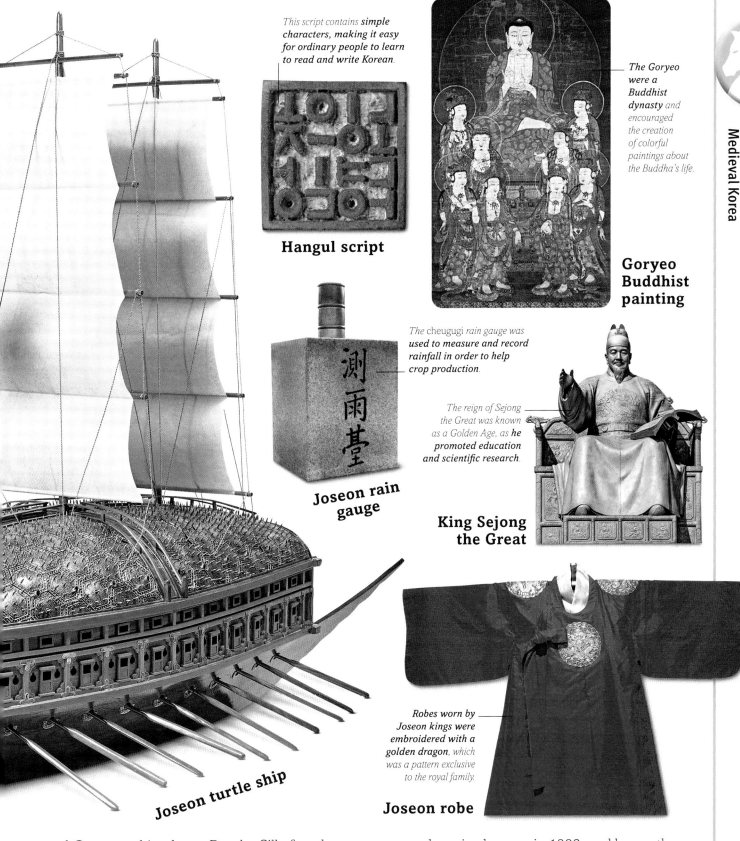

*This script contains **simple characters**, making it easy for ordinary people to learn to read and write Korean.*

Hangul script

*The Goryeo were a **Buddhist dynasty** and encouraged the creation of colorful paintings about the Buddha's life.*

Goryeo Buddhist painting

*The cheugugi rain gauge was **used to measure and record rainfall** in order to help crop production.*

Joseon rain gauge

*The reign of Sejong the Great was known as a Golden Age, as **he promoted education and scientific research**.*

King Sejong the Great

*Robes worn by Joseon kings were **embroidered with a golden dragon**, which was a pattern exclusive to the royal family.*

Joseon robe

Joseon turtle ship

and Goguryeo kingdoms. But the Silla faced resistance to their rule because of the strict class system they imposed, and they were overthrown by the Goryeo in 918. The Goryeo period is known for the creation of high-quality **celadon pottery** and vibrant **Buddhist paintings**. Taejo—a former Goryeo military general—seized power in 1388, and began the Joseon Dynasty in 1392. The Joseon period saw advances in science and learning, such as the invention of the **rain gauge**. Joseon ruler **Sejong the Great** also created the **Hangul script**, which is still used today in Korea.

Medieval Japan

*Built in 607 during the Asuka period, this Buddhist temple complex **contains some of the oldest wooden buildings in the world.***

*Buddhism was the main religion of Japan by the Heian period, and many temples had statues of **Amida Nyorai or Amitābha—the Buddha of Limitless Light.***

Buddhism

The Tale of Genji

Often regarded as the world's first novel, The Tale of Genji follows the life of a fictional emperor's son.

Hōryū-ji temple

Minamoto Yoritomo set up Japan's first shogunate (government led by a shogun), in Kamakura, a coastal city to the south of modern-day Tokyo.

Amida Nyorai rules over a heaven called the **Western Pure Land**.

Minamoto Yoritomo

Japan had a strict social hierarchy in which the shogun and daimyo were granted the most honorable status, followed by the samurai, peasants, craftworkers, and merchants.

Daimyo and samurai

The Mongols tried to invade Japan in 1274 and 1281, but their attempts were hampered by typhoons that were called kamikaze, meaning "divine winds."

Mongol attacks on Japan

*After six hours of fighting, the forces of Tokugawa Ieyasu emerged victorious, **bringing an end to a period of bloody conflict.***

The period from 538 to 1185 in Japan is known for the spread of Buddhism, and as the high point of imperial court life. By the end of the 12th century, political power began to shift from the emperor to shoguns (military leaders), who spent the next few centuries wrestling for control of the region.

During the Heian period in Japan (794–1185), the emperor's court at Kyoto was run by nobles, while the shoguns kept the peace in the provinces. Painting and writing flourished at court, with artists like Murasaki Shikibu producing works such as *The Tale of Genji*. However, as the emperor's power declined, the shoguns began competing for control

Shinobi

*More than 80 buildings make up this castle in Himeji, Japan, which **served as the center of feudal power for several shoguns**.*

*The **O-yoroi** (armor) **of the samurai** covered them from head to toe and was made of iron and leather plates.*

Himeji-jo castle

The shinobi *were trained to be stealthy and were used for spying and assassinations.*

Onna-musha (female warriors), such as Hangaku Gozen, fought along with the samurai in the wars between the different shoguns.

Oda Nobunaga was a daimyo who tried to unify Japan, equipping his samurai with firearms to get the upper hand in battle.

Oda Nobunaga

Hangaku Gozen

Samurai armor

Battle of Sekigahara

and territory, using armies of skilled warriors called **samurai**. In 1185, the samurai **Minamoto Yoritomo** set up a new capital in Kamakura. From here he sought to control Japan, and even repelled two **Mongol attacks**. Under Japan's feudal system, shoguns delegated military power to daimyo (landowning nobles). Rival shoguns continued to fight each other, until daimyo **Oda Nobunaga** began unifying the warring factions in 1560. After his death in 1582, a power struggle broke out, leading to the **Battle of Sekigahara**. This battle ended in victory for warlord Tokugawa Ieyasu, who unified Japan under his rule.

Medieval warfare

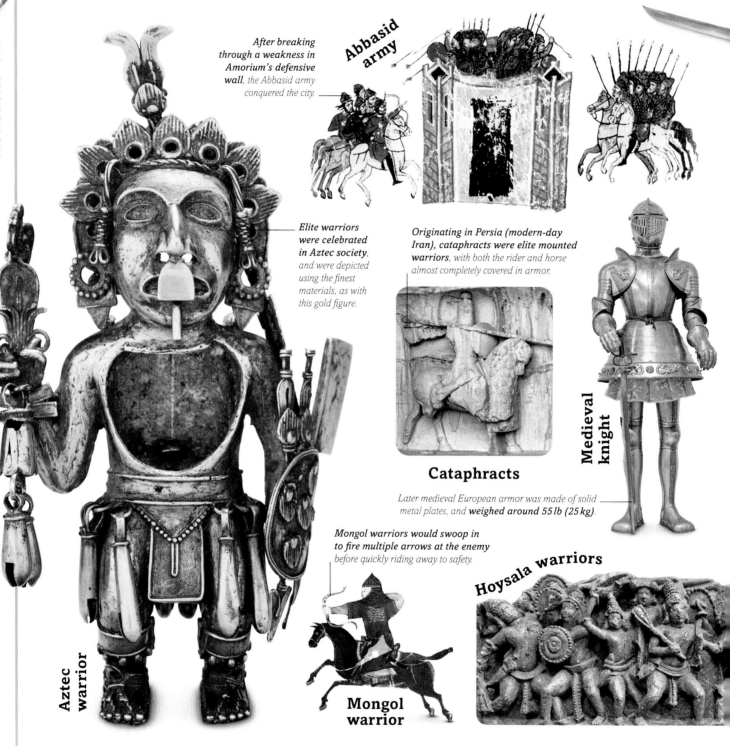

After breaking through a weakness in Amorium's defensive wall, the Abbasid army conquered the city.

Abbasid army

Elite warriors were celebrated in Aztec society, and were depicted using the finest materials, as with this gold figure.

Originating in Persia (modern-day Iran), cataphracts were elite mounted warriors, with both the rider and horse almost completely covered in armor.

Cataphracts

Medieval knight

Later medieval European armor was made of solid metal plates, and weighed around 55 lb (25 kg).

Mongol warriors would swoop in to fire multiple arrows at the enemy before quickly riding away to safety.

Aztec warrior

Mongol warrior

Hoysala warriors

The millennium following 500 CE was a period of violent unrest in many parts of the world as rulers clashed over territory, religious beliefs, and various other issues. Armies employed well-trained warriors and creative military tacticians to find the best ways to crush their enemies in battle.

Warriors risked their lives in long, brutal battles, and were celebrated for their courage, as seen in the illustrations of the **Abbasid army** capturing the city of Amorium (in what is now Turkey) in 838 CE. Weapons such as sharp **pikes**, deadly **Viking axes**, and heavy **Chinese iron maces** could inflict horrific injuries. To protect themselves

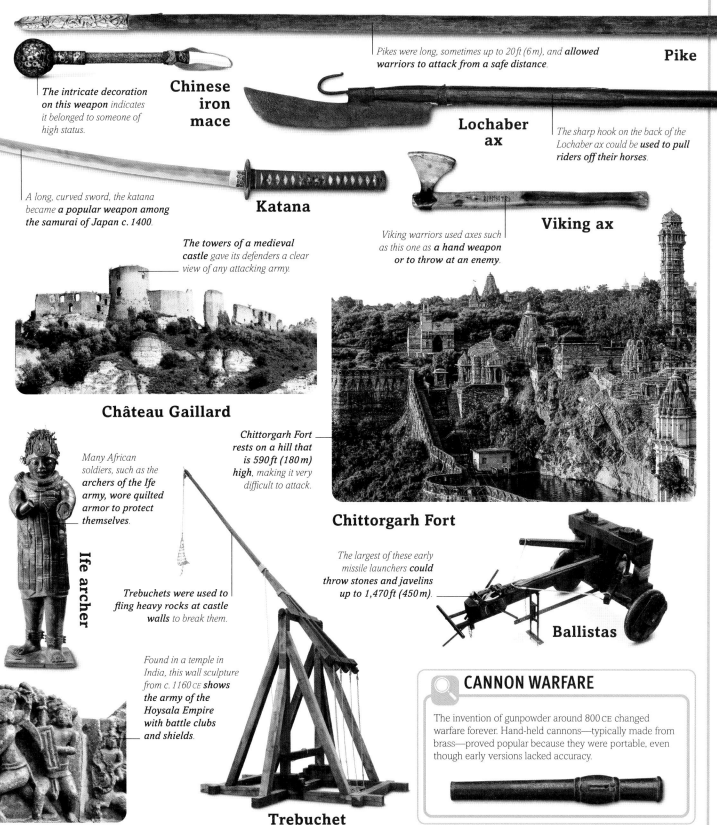

Chinese iron mace

The intricate decoration on this weapon indicates it belonged to someone of high status.

*Pikes were long, sometimes up to 20 ft (6 m), and **allowed warriors to attack from a safe distance**.*

Pike

Lochaber ax

*The sharp hook on the back of the Lochaber ax could be **used to pull riders off their horses**.*

Katana

*A long, curved sword, the katana became **a popular weapon among the samurai of Japan c. 1400**.*

Viking ax

*Viking warriors used axes such as this one as **a hand weapon or to throw at an enemy**.*

The towers of a medieval castle gave its defenders a clear view of any attacking army.

Château Gaillard

*Many African soldiers, such as the **archers of the Ife army**, wore quilted armor to protect themselves.*

Ife archer

Chittorgarh Fort rests on a hill that is 590 ft (180 m) high, making it very difficult to attack.

Chittorgarh Fort

*The largest of these early missile launchers **could throw stones and javelins up to 1,470 ft (450 m)**.*

Ballistas

Trebuchets were used to fling heavy rocks at castle walls to break them.

*Found in a temple in India, this wall sculpture from c. 1160 CE **shows the army of the Hoysala Empire with battle clubs and shields**.*

CANNON WARFARE

The invention of gunpowder around 800 CE changed warfare forever. Hand-held cannons—typically made from brass—proved popular because they were portable, even though early versions lacked accuracy.

Trebuchet

on the battlefield, soldiers such as **knights** and **cataphracts** wore strong armor. Rulers kept their families safe inside forts and castles such as the French **Château Gaillard**. However, the invention of war machines like the **trebuchet** allowed attacking armies to launch objects over castle walls. Some rulers built forts on high ground to withstand such attacks, such as the 7th-century **Chittorgarh Fort** in India, which is on top of a steep hill, with high walls. Yet few buildings could hold out against the explosive power of the cannon. Towns fell much more easily now, as they could not hold out through lengthy sieges.

Tang and Song China

Emperor Taizong

Throughout the Tang and Song dynasties, candidates were tested on a range of subjects, from Confucian philosophy to history and literature, with the top scorers gaining high positions in the imperial government.

The bright, colorful glaze on pottery, as seen on this female figure at the Tang imperial court, was an important development in Chinese ceramics.

Taking over from his father, Emperor Gaozu, in 626, Taizong reigned over a period of peace and prosperity.

Civil service

Tang ceramics

Longmen Grottoes

Around 110,000 Buddhist statues were carved from stone during the Tang Dynasty and line the Longmen Grottoes in Henan province, China.

Li Bai

Li Bai wrote more than 1,000 poems on different themes, including the natural world and friendship.

> Tang ceramics are known for their **tricolor glazes** of yellow, green, and brown.

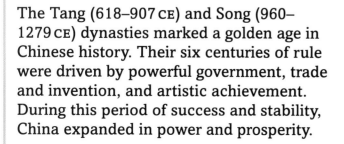

The Tang (618–907 CE) and Song (960–1279 CE) dynasties marked a golden age in Chinese history. Their six centuries of rule were driven by powerful government, trade and invention, and artistic achievement. During this period of success and stability, China expanded in power and prosperity.

The Tang Dynasty got underway when regional governor Li Yuan took charge as the first emperor. He was followed by his son Li Shimin, known as **Emperor Taizong**, who became one of the greatest emperors in China's history. The Tang Empire and government grew stronger and larger by using an examination system that ensured only

Song cities

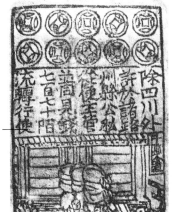

This panoramic scroll painting of the Song capital city of Bianjing (modern-day Kaifeng) shows the city being expanded to support the booming population.

*In 1127, after the northern Song capital of Bianjing fell to the Jurchen Jin Dynasty, **Emperor Gaozong established the southern Song Empire and eventually settled in Lin'an (present-day Hangzhou).***

*Chinese sailing ships, or junks, had **watertight compartments to protect cargo.***

*Introduced in the 11th century, **Song paper currency or** jiaozi **were the first bank notes in history**.*

Emperor Gaozong of Song

Song paper money

SONG INVENTIONS

During the Song Dynasty, China was a leader in groundbreaking technologies. New inventions included gunpowder for explosive fireworks; the nautical compass featuring a magnetized iron needle for navigation; and the astronomical clock to tell the time, date, and phases of the moon.

Gunpowder

Magnetic compass

Astronomical clock

Model of Song sailing ship

Packs of 30 cardboard playing cards were used for games at the Song court.

Playing cards

the best candidates entered **the civil service. Tang ceramics**, painting, and sculpture also flourished, and poets such as **Li Bai** captured the positive atmosphere of the time in their writing. However, the Tang Dynasty ended in disharmony, with China being divided into separate kingdoms. Unity was restored under the Song Dynasty

in 960. **Song cities** thrived, with the empire's population doubling to 100 million people. **Song sailing ships** traded goods in distant lands and **Song paper money** became the world's first paper currency. The Song were invaded by the Mongols, who established the Yuan Dynasty.

Southeast Asian kingdoms

The faces of gods and goddesses *decorated the outsides of Cham temples.*

Lord Shiva can be recognized by the third eye in **the middle** of his forehead.

Head of Shiva

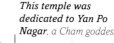

Buddhist deities, such as **this bodhisattva** *(person on the path to enlightenment), were worshipped in the Cham kingdom.*

This temple was dedicated to Yan Po **Nagar**, *a Cham goddess.*

Po Nagar

Bodhisattva

Sandstone sculptures of **mythical creatures** *were placed at the entrances of Cham temples.*

Sandstone dragon

Temples of Bagan

KINGDOMS OF SOUTHEAST ASIA

The Khmer kingdom controlled much of modern-day Cambodia, while the Pagan ruled Myanmar. Much of northern Vietnam was under Dai Viet control, but the southern part was ruled by the Cham kingdom.

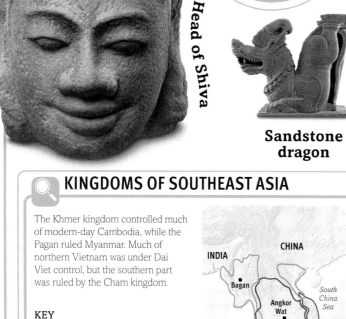

CHINA
INDIA
Bagan
Angkor Wat
South China Sea
Gulf of Thailand

KEY

— Pagan kingdom

— Khmer kingdom

— Cham kingdom

— Dai Viet kingdom

From the 2nd century CE, wealthy kingdoms emerged in Southeast Asia on the trade and religious pilgrimage routes between China and India. These included the Khmer (802–1431), the Pagan (849–1297), the Dai Viet (968–1804), and the Cham (192–1832).

The Hindu rulers of the Khmer kingdom built temples to Hindu gods, such as at **Angkor Wat**, and also portrayed themselves as god-kings. Some later rulers adopted Buddhism, but continued to present themselves as divine, such as King Jayavarman VII, who had his own face engraved onto the Buddhist **Bayon temples**. In Myanmar,

Life of the Buddha

Pagan sculptures often depicted scenes from the life of the Buddha.

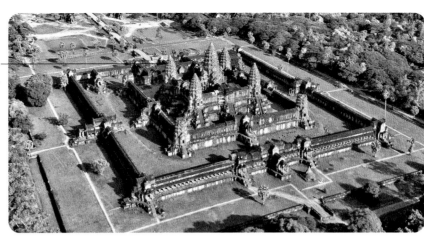

The five temple towers symbolize the peaks of Mount Meru, the home of the gods in Hinduism.

Angkor Wat

*The stone towers of the Bayon temples are carved with **216 smiling faces**.*

Bayon temples

*The almond-shaped eyes of Dai Viet sculptures show the **influence of Chinese artistic styles**.*

This Dai Viet pagoda was built on a single stone pillar and resembles a lotus flower rising out of the water.

Nearly 10,000 Buddhist temples and pagodas were built at Bagan, of which fewer than a quarter have survived.

One Pillar Pagoda

*Dai Viet pottery was often **decorated** with pictures of wild animals and birds.*

Storage Jar

Buddha rising up from the lotus

*Tran Quoc Tang was a Dai Viet **general** who fought off two invasions by the more powerful Mongol army.*

Tran Quoc Tang

the Indigenous peoples were united under Pagan rule that lasted for nearly 250 years. During this time, the Pagan kings built thousands of Buddhist **temples in Bagan**. Their rule was destroyed by the Mongols, who also tried to conquer the Dai Viet kingdom, but failed. The Dai Viet were heavily influenced by Chinese art and architecture. Farther south, the Cham kingdom's access to the sea and its trade in spices and silk made it very wealthy. Most Cham kings were Hindu and built **sandstone structures** dedicated to **Lord Shiva**.

85

Polynesian great voyages

Outrigger canoe

Developed centuries ago, these canoes are still used by the Polynesians—the support float on one side keeps the vessel stable on the waves.

The sailors followed birds, such as the white tern, which flew out to sea in the morning and back to land at night.

Flight patterns of birds

*With more space between the hulls to carry supplies and goods, **these large canoes allowed groups and families to make long voyages to new islands.***

The travelers memorized the fixed positions of the stars to sail at night.

*Bananas, yam, flour, and sweet potatoes **were stored for ocean journeys,** while spears were used to catch fish, turtles, and crabs.*

Food for voyages

Positions of the stars

Double-hulled canoe

*Constructed between the 11th and 17th centuries, **the moai stand with their backs to the sea, watching over the people of Rapa Nui.***

POLYNESIAN TRIANGLE

Around the triangular region of Polynesia in the central Pacific Ocean sit the Hawaiian Islands in the north, New Zealand in the west, and Rapa Nui (Easter Island) in the east. The region includes more than 1,000 islands, and the countries located here include Tuvalu, Samoa, Tonga, and French Polynesia.

Pacific Ocean

Coral Sea

AUSTRALIA

KEY

  Polynesia

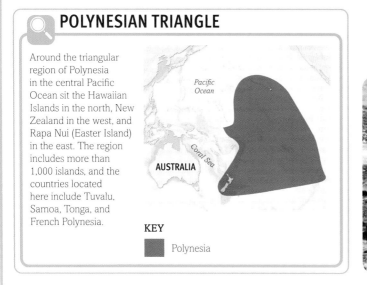

From 3000 BCE, sailors from Southeast Asian islands set out to find new lands. Known as the Lapita people, they settled on islands such as Vanuatu and Fiji in the central Pacific. From here they continued to explore farther, reaching nearly all Pacific islands by around 1200 CE, when they discovered New Zealand.

The sailors journeyed to the islands on vessels such as **outrigger canoes** and **double-hulled canoes**, which were joined together using planks. They navigated on the open seas by observing the **flight patterns of birds** and the **positions of the stars**. Their travels also helped them understand the routes between the islands, which

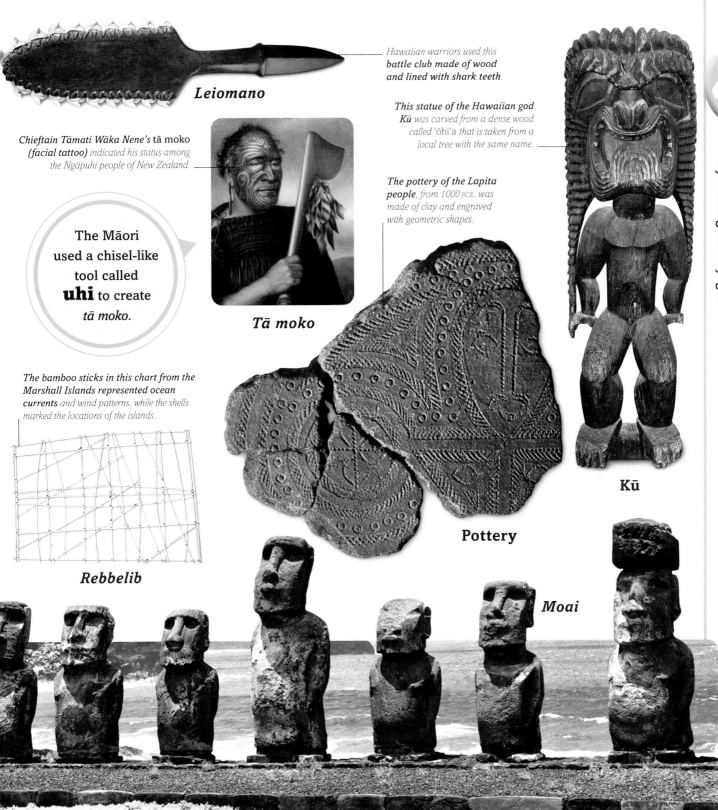

Hawaiian warriors used this battle club made of wood and lined with shark teeth.

Leiomano

Chieftain Tāmati Wāka Nene's tā moko (facial tattoo) indicated his status among the Ngāpuhi people of New Zealand.

This statue of the Hawaiian god Kū was carved from a dense wood called 'ōhi'a that is taken from a local tree with the same name.

The Māori used a chisel-like tool called **uhi** to create *tā moko.*

The pottery of the Lapita people, from 1000 BCE, was made of clay and engraved with geometric shapes.

Tā moko

The bamboo sticks in this chart from the Marshall Islands represented ocean currents and wind patterns, while the shells marked the locations of the islands.

Kū

Rebbelib

Pottery

Moai

they recorded through bamboo-stick maps called ***rebbelib***. In Polynesia, the groups of travelers settled on parts of individual islands or across series of islands. Over time, a diverse range of cultures developed across this region as each group developed their own way of life, customs, and religious beliefs. The Hawaiians worshipped Kū, their god of war, farming, and fishing, while the people of Rapa Nui (Easter Island) built giant statues called ***moai*** to represent their ancestors. In New Zealand, body art, such as ***tā moko*** (facial tattoos), was used to indicate a person's tribe, rank in society, and victories in war.

Maya, Aztec, and Inca

Maya limestone carving

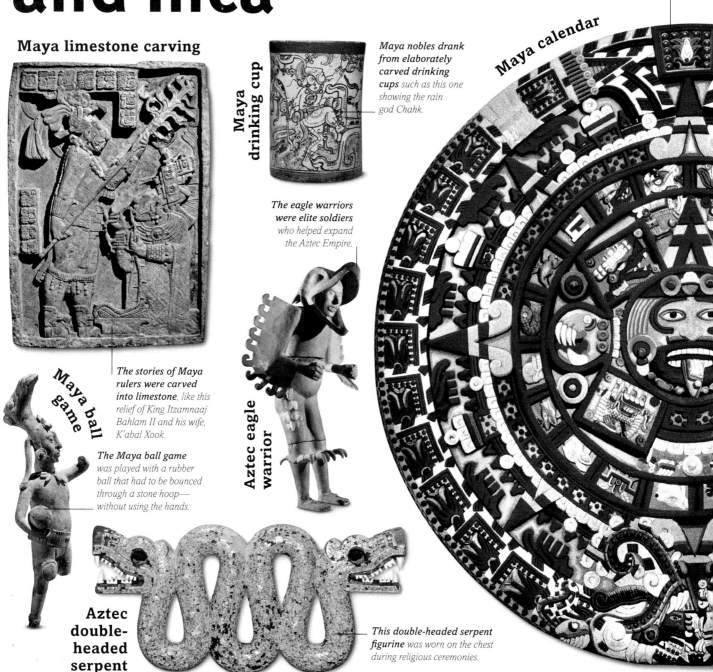

*The Maya have many different calendars, such as **the Tzolk'in**, which tracks religious festivals.*

Maya calendar

Maya drinking cup

Maya nobles drank from elaborately carved drinking cups such as this one showing the rain god Chahk.

The eagle warriors were elite soldiers who helped expand the Aztec Empire.

Maya ball game

The stories of Maya rulers were carved into limestone, like this relief of King Itzamnaaj Bahlam II and his wife, K'abal Xook.

The Maya ball game was played with a rubber ball that had to be bounced through a stone hoop— without using the hands.

Aztec eagle warrior

Aztec double-headed serpent

This double-headed serpent figurine was worn on the chest during religious ceremonies.

The Maya, Aztec, and Inca were great civilizations that flourished in Central and South America. They built empires that ruled over millions of people. Although these empires collapsed or were destroyed by European invaders, the descendants of their people still continue their cultures.

The Maya civilization reached the height of its power and influence between 250 CE and 950 CE. During this time, the Maya had more than 40 cities, with thousands of residents. These cities were full of temples and palaces decorated with **carvings**, and courts for playing **ball games**. After 950 CE, the Maya civilization collapsed, partly due to

Huitzilopochtli

Huitzilopochtli, also known as the Turquoise Prince, was one of the two main deities the Aztecs worshipped.

*Made from the bright blue and green feathers of rainforest birds, **Aztec** headdresses were worn in religious ceremonies.*

Only **nobles, warriors,** and **priests** could wear feather headdresses.

Aztec headdress

Masks made of gold were designed to cover the faces of rulers and nobles after their deaths as a part of burial rituals.

This ancient city contains more than 150 buildings, including houses, palaces, temples, and burial grounds.

Inca mask

The animals on this Inca bowl represent the different parts of the Inca Empire—the seabird for the ocean, the llama for the Andes mountains, and the cat for the rainforest.

Inca pottery

Machu Picchu

drought and war, and its people abandoned the cities. In the 14th century, a wandering tribe called the Aztecs settled in modern-day Mexico and went on to build a vast empire. Their main god, **Huitzilopochtli**, was often shown as an eagle or a hummingbird, and so **Aztec warriors** wore uniforms resembling eagles and their nobles and priests wore **feather headdresses**. In South America, the Inca Empire rose up in the 15th century in the Andes mountains and expanded its rule with military force. The Inca built many cities, such as **Machu Picchu**, and created intricate craftwork, including gold **masks** and **pottery**.

MESOAMERICAN PYRAMIDS
The ancient Mesoamerican civilizations were home to master builders who constructed great pyramids in the heart of their communities and cities. Made from soil and stone, these carefully crafted creations, such as Kukulcán in the Maya city of Chichén Itzá, Mexico, were the sacred centers of public life.

Mesoamerica is a cultural area extending from central Mexico to Costa Rica, and was home to many great civilizations such as the Olmecs, Aztecs, and Maya. These cultures lived in sprawling cities filled with markets, houses, and plazas—at the center of which was a stepped pyramid made of stone blocks. The pyramid steps usually led to a temple, shrine, or platform at the top, where priests carried out rituals in honor of the gods. Some Mesoamerican cultures also buried their rulers inside the pyramids. Many pyramids built by these civilizations still stand today as a testament to the creativity of their people.

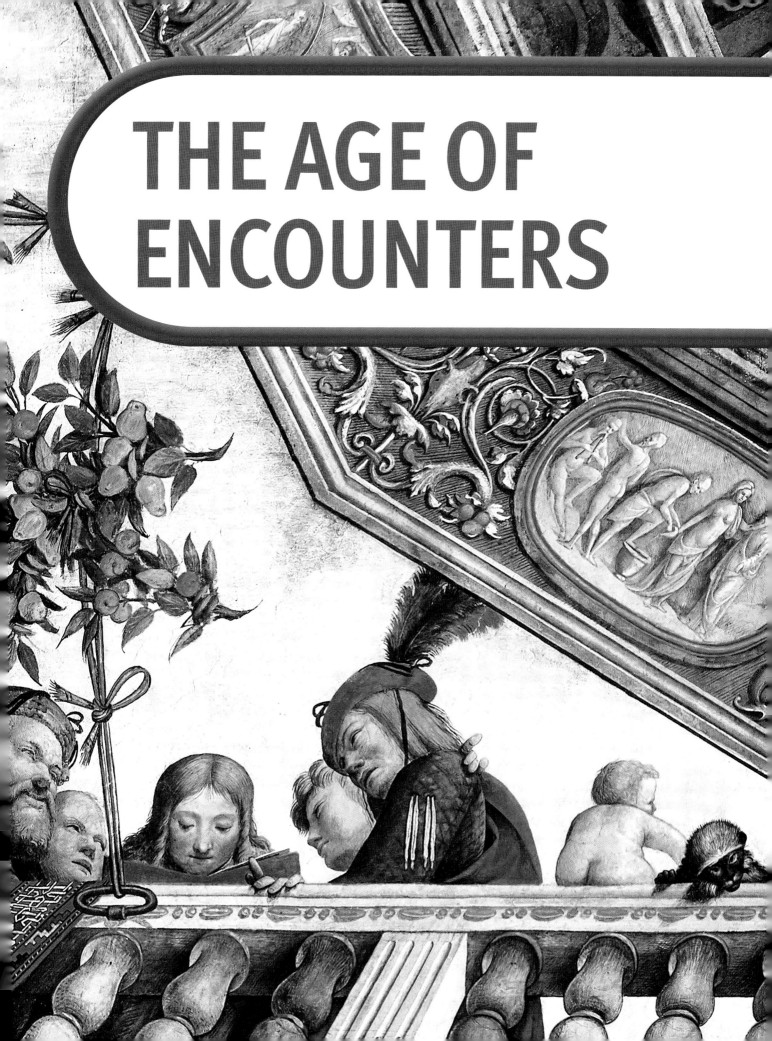

THE AGE OF ENCOUNTERS

The Age of Encounters

Europe's first contact with cultures across the Atlantic Ocean in 1492 led to the exploitation of American lands and peoples, and the enslavement of millions of Africans, as Europe built empires to rival those of China, India, and the Middle East.

Between the late 15th and early 18th centuries, the world seemed to become much smaller as sailors opened up new sea routes and mapped previously uncharted lands. Europe was at the forefront of this age of exploration, spurred on by a spirit of curiosity and the search for new trade routes. This era of discovery was not restricted to exploration of the globe, however, as scientists made a series of revolutionary discoveries that changed how people thought about the world around them.

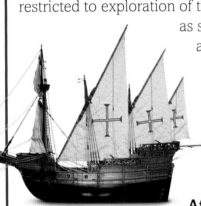

CARAVEL
In the 15th century, Portugal developed new sailing vessels to explore the coast of Africa and the Atlantic Ocean. The small size of these caravels made them maneuverable, and the lateen (triangular) sails gave them great speed.

African trade

New ship designs allowed Europeans to explore the coast of Africa as they searched for a sea route to India. This increased contact between European nations and wealthy African peoples, such as the Kingdom of Benin and the Kingdom of Kongo in West and Southwest Africa. As Europeans and Africans expanded their trade with each other, Europeans introduced Christianity to the region. This period also saw the beginning of the Atlantic slave trade, in which more than 12 million Africans were forcibly transported to European colonies in the Americas. Most of those who survived the journey went on to endure lives of great hardship on plantations.

The Islamic world

While Europeans introduced Christianity into the Americas and parts of Africa south of the Sahara, the Islamic world continued to flourish and expand. Three great Islamic empires arose during this period: the Ottomans in parts of the Middle East,

BUST OF AN IYOBA
In the Kingdom of Benin, the iyoba was the mother of the oba (king). Iyoba were considered powerful protectors of the kingdom.

HUMAYUN'S TOMB
The tomb of the second Mughal emperor, Humayun, was constructed in 1558 at the center of a paradise garden in Delhi, India. This grand mausoleum complex set the style for later Mughal tombs, including the massive Taj Mahal built by the emperor Shah Jahan.

the eastern Mediterranean, and North Africa; the Safavids across parts of the Middle East and Central Asia; and the Mughals in South Asia. All three were powerful empires, leaving behind a legacy of stunning architecture, scientific advancements, and beautiful works of art.

Stability in East Asia

To the east, the empire of China continued to thrive under the Ming Dynasty (1368–1644), which oversaw a number of grand engineering projects, including the maintaining and strengthening of the Great Wall; dredging the entire length of the world's longest human-made waterway, the Grand Canal in eastern China; and building the Forbidden City in the capital, Beijing. When the Ming Dynasty collapsed, the empire continued under the Qing Dynasty, who went on to rule China until the early 20th century.

East of China, Japan was finally unified in the 17th century under the Tokugawa Shogunate. Its shoguns ruled from a new capital at Edo (modern-day Tokyo). Japan had little contact with the outside world during this Edo period, which was a time of great peace, prosperity, and artistic and cultural achievement.

Destruction in the Americas

In contrast to East Asia's period of relative peace, on the other side of the world, many American cultures that had survived for centuries collapsed after contact with European explorers. Spanish conquistadors led their armies to the Americas, plundering civilizations such as the Aztecs and the Inca. Even settlers who had no plans of conquest brought death with them, introducing new diseases to the Americas that killed off large portions of the Indigenous populations. Yet stories of the wealth that could be found or made in the new lands continued to entice hundreds of thousands of Europeans to make the voyage over the Atlantic to start a new life in the Americas.

ATAHUALPA
The last Inca emperor to hold any real power, Atahualpa was captured and imprisoned by Spanish conquistadors, and eventually executed.

THE GREAT WALL OF CHINA
A wall along the northern border of China was constructed by the first emperor, Qin Shi Huangdi, in the 3rd century BCE, though little now survives. The Great Wall as we know it today was rebuilt during the Ming Dynasty, both to defend the empire and to control trade.

Ottomans and Safavids

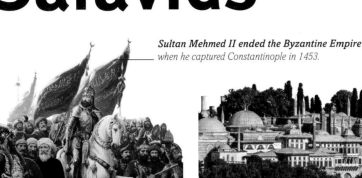

Sultan Mehmed II ended the Byzantine Empire when he captured Constantinople in 1453.

Suleiman's helmet was made of gold and decorated with precious stones including rubies and turquoise.

As well as being the home and court of the sultan, Topkapi Palace held the royal treasury and a grand library.

Topkapi Palace

The fall of Constantinople

Helmet of Suleiman the Magnificent

Coffee houses became popular in the Ottoman Empire after the beverage was introduced in the 16th century.

Geography box

Coffee house

A kiblenüma (compass in Turkish) was used to find the direction of Mecca, so that a Muslim could pray while facing the holy city.

The Janissaries were the sultan's personal bodyguards and among the empire's most effective soldiers.

Hürrem Sultan

An enslaved girl from Ukraine, Hürrem Sultan became the queen of the Ottomans when she married Emperor Suleiman.

Janissary guards

The Ottomans and Safavids were powerful rival Islamic empires between the 16th and 18th centuries. Each empire considered itself to be the true leader of all Muslims, and created its own distinct styles of Islamic art and architecture.

After the **fall of Constantinople** to the Ottomans in 1453, the city was renamed Istanbul and became the capital of their empire. The city's **Topkapi Palace** was the home and court of the sultan, while the streets were policed by elite

Persian carpet

The use of silk threads and colored dyes made Safavid Persian carpets extremely popular around the world.

In 2011, a single page of the *Shahnameh* was sold for about **$10 million** at auction.

A poem written by the 10th-century Persian poet Ferdowsi, the Shahnameh (Book of Kings) *was illustrated with miniature paintings.*

Paradise gardens

Safavid paradise gardens were designed in the "Chahar Bagh" pattern, a layout where walkways or waterways divided the garden into four parts.

The *Shahnameh*

Also known as Abbas the Great, Shah Abbas I recovered a lot of Safavid territory that had been lost under previous rulers.

Shah Abbas I

🔍 THE OTTOMAN AND SAFAVID EMPIRES

At its peak, the Ottoman Empire ruled over territories on three continents—parts of Europe, North Africa, and western Asia. Safavid rule spread across Central Asia up to parts of modern-day Pakistan. The two rivals fought many times over Mesopotamia (present-day Iraq).

EUROPE
ASIA
MESOPOTAMIA
AFRICA

KEY

— Ottoman Empire c. 1683   — Safavid Empire c. 1512

After it was finished in 1629, the Shah Mosque was the tallest building in Isfahan.

Shah Mosque, Isfahan

Janissary guards. At the height of Ottoman power, the empire was ruled by Suleiman the Magnificent, with his queen, **Hürrem Sultan**, by his side. Shortly after Suleiman's death, the Safavid Empire of Persia (present-day Iran) saw a golden age under **Shah Abbas I**. He commissioned buildings adorned with colorful tiles and calligraphy, such as the **Shah Mosque** in the capital, Isfahan. Gardens were designed to match the **paradise gardens** in the Qur'an, the holy book of Islam. The Safavid Dynasty was ousted from power in the early 18th century, but the rivalry between the Ottomans and Persia continued.

ISLAMIC ART
From the 7th century onward, Muslim conquests spread the religion of Islam from the Arabian peninsula across Asia and Africa. As a result, many different regions became somewhat united by a shared faith. They developed common Islamic styles and influences that could be seen across art, architecture, and culture. Many of these early Islamic styles remain popular today.

The painting above is part of a manuscript from Persia (modern-day Iran) that tells the love story of King Khosrow II and Shirin—the main character and the future queen of Persia. It is an excellent example of Islamic miniature painting, which became a key feature of Persian and Ottoman art by the 14th century. These elaborate, small paintings usually came from larger manuscripts or book illustrations, and became famous for their vibrant colors, intricate details on clothes, and geometric shapes in repeated patterns. These shapes are an important feature of Islamic art and are also found on ceramics and the walls of Islamic homes and mosques.

The Renaissance

Dutch philosopher Erasmus was a key humanist who believed that people had free will.

Erasmus

Florence Cathedral

The dome of this Italian cathedral was designed by Renaissance architect Filippo Brunelleschi in the 15th century.

The lute was the most popular musical instrument in Renaissance Europe.

Renaissance lute

The School of Athens

Leonardo da Vinci's painting of Jesus with his followers was created for a church in Milan in the 1490s.

The Last Supper

Michelangelo's marble sculpture of the Biblical figure David was inspired by the art of ancient Greece and Rome.

Pearl-adorned gold jewelery was popular among wealthy women during this period.

This painting, created by Raphael, shows many of the great thinkers of ancient Greece.

David

Boat-shaped pendant

Lasting from the 14th to 17th centuries, the Renaissance was a period of rapid change and incredible creativity in Europe. Artists and writers rediscovered the art, architecture, and values of ancient Greece and Rome, while thinkers and scientists challenged the teachings of the Church and began to unlock the secrets of the universe. This period produced some of the most stunning artwork, challenging philosophy, and magnificent architecture in the history of Europe.

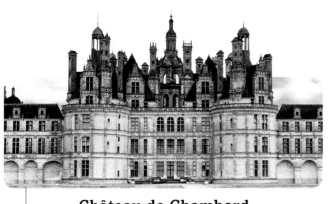

Château de Chambord

This vast French castle, built during the 16th century, is one of the finest Renaissance buildings.

Isaac Newton created the first reflecting telescope, which used mirrors instead of lenses, in 1668.

Newton's telescope

Italian artist Artemisia Gentileschi was a successful Renaissance painter, at a time when art was considered to be a profession for men alone.

Self-portrait by Artemisia Gentileschi

Polish astronomer Nicolaus Copernicus used math to work out that Earth revolves around the sun.

Copernican model of the solar system

It took the artist Raphael more than **three years** to finish this painting.

Jan van Eyck, from the Netherlands, refined the technique of oil painting during the 15th century.

Jan van Eyck

Martin Luther translated the Bible into German and challenged the power of the Roman Catholic Church.

Das Alte Testa ment deutsch. M. Luther. Dvittemberg.

Page from Luther's German Bible

During the Renaissance, humanists such as **Erasmus**, inspired by the ideals of the ancient world, challenged the traditional beliefs of the time. Others, too, began to think more critically about the world around them. For instance, **Copernicus** calculated that Earth orbited the sun (and not the other way around). The printing press allowed new ideas to spread quickly—the mass printing of Martin Luther's **German Bible** helped his ideas reach more people. Interest in ancient Greece and Rome also inspired artists—Michelangelo created his sculpture of **David**, and Raphael painted his fresco **The School of Athens**. At the same time, elaborate buildings, such as **Florence Cathedral** and the **Château de Chambord**, were being built across Europe.

Books and printing

*In Mesopotamia, cylinder seals were **used to stamp personal items and as legal seals for documents**.*

Cylinder seal

Indus Valley seal

Indus Valley merchants stamped their trade goods with seals like this one, which depicts an ancient god wrestling two tigers.

The Book of Kells

*The oldest papyrus document ever found **describes the construction of the Great Pyramid of Giza in Egypt.***

Papyri of Pharaoh Khufu

Only three complete Maya codices survive today.

Written on papyrus scrolls, the Book of the Dead *was placed in ancient Egyptian tombs and **contained spells to help guide the souls of the dead to the afterlife.***

Book of the Dead

Madrid Codex

The earliest forms of writing began more than 5,000 years ago in ancient Mesopotamia. Over time, new developments—including printing—transformed the importance of writing in cultures around the world. The invention of the printing press allowed books to be mass-produced for millions of readers.

Many ancient civilizations found ways to keep records in their communities. In ancient Egypt, hieroglyphic writings on papyrus sheets were used to document local records and religious works, such as the ***Book of the Dead***. The Sumerians of Mesopotamia adopted soft clay tablets for writing and stone **cylinder seals** to stamp goods and

The Diamond Sutra, *a Buddhist manuscript dating back to 868 CE, is the **world's oldest surviving complete book**.*

Diamond Sutra

These 18th-century Chinese printing blocks contain carved raised letters, which were placed in ink before being pressed onto paper.

Movable printing blocks

*Built by German inventor Johannes Gutenberg, this press **used oil-based ink and mechanical movable type to print books**.*

Jain manuscript

*Jain manuscripts were written on **dried palm leaves** and held together by a string through the middle.*

Jikji

A religious work from 1377 by a Korean Buddhist monk, the Jikji was among the first books to be printed with movable metal type.

Gutenberg printing press

Hardback books

*Mass-produced paper books in hardback and paperback **are affordable formats** that can entertain and educate readers of all ages.*

*The Madrid Codex contains **details of Maya religious rituals meant to guide priests**.*

*Invented in 1997, these devices can make thousands of books and newspapers available to **read on a screen at the press of a button**.*

E-reader

documents. In China, papermaking was invented, as well as **movable printing blocks**. In many cultures, early texts were written or printed on scrolls, but these were eventually replaced by folded formats that were easier to read and carry. By medieval times, important books, such as *The Book of Kells,* contained handwritten text and elaborate pictures. The Aztecs and Maya created similar folding books, such as the **Madrid Codex**. In the 15th century, the invention of the **Gutenberg printing press** in Europe made printing faster and easier. Today, we can read in many formats, including on digital devices such as **e-readers**.

Advances in warfare

Arquebus gun

Pike and shot

*At the Battle of Pavia in 1525, German and Italian forces used **formations of soldiers armed with pikes and firearms to great effect**.*

The Safavids of Iran used long guns to help subdue any neighboring groups to their rising new empire.

Safavid musketeer

In 1453, the Ottoman army fired iron balls from massive cannons at the walls of Constantinople for 55 days until the city fell, marking the end of the Byzantine Empire.

Ottoman cannon

Unlike earlier firing weapons, which were large and heavy, the arquebus gun only weighed about 13 lb (6 kg) and could be carried by infantry soldiers onto the battlefield.

*A gun introduced to Japan by the Portuguese, the Tanegashima was **used by noble samurai warriors and their foot soldiers**.*

Gunpowder was carried in specially designed containers, such as this elaborate flask from the Mughal Empire.

Gunpowder flask

Tanegashima

In the 15th century, weapons that used gunpowder to fire at the enemy became more common on the battlefield. These firearms could cause devastation on a wider scale than earlier weapons. Victory now came to lie with those who could use this power effectively.

Medieval battle tactics began to change, with the addition of firearms creating formidable **pike and shot** formations. Gunpowder weapons like the **arquebus gun** were used by European armies, the Ottomans, and the Mughals to expand their territories. Large and powerful **cannons** could break down the fortified walls and gates of a barricaded city, quickly ending a siege. By the

Demi-cannons were used by both sides in the four Anglo-Dutch naval wars from 1652 to 1784.

Demi-cannons, Anglo-Dutch naval wars

Demi-cannons were kept in the **lower decks** and fired at enemy ships as they got close.

*This cannon was easy to load and **could be rotated to fire in quick succession in many directions**.*

Breech-loading swivel gun

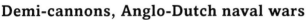

Brown Bess musket

*The Brown Bess was not very accurate, but it could fire up to four shots per minute, making it **effective when used by a large group of infantry firing at close range**.*

Moukhala musket

*Made in the 17th century in **Morocco, Algeria, and Tunisia**, this long-barrel musket was used in nearly all North African wars until the 20th century.*

*Flintlock pistols, such as this one from Scotland, were **smaller guns that could be used both for self-defense in private life as well as in battle**.*

Bayonet

Flintlock pistol

A bayonet was a knife or dagger at the end of a firearm, which was used to attack once the gun ran out of gunpowder or if the enemy was close.

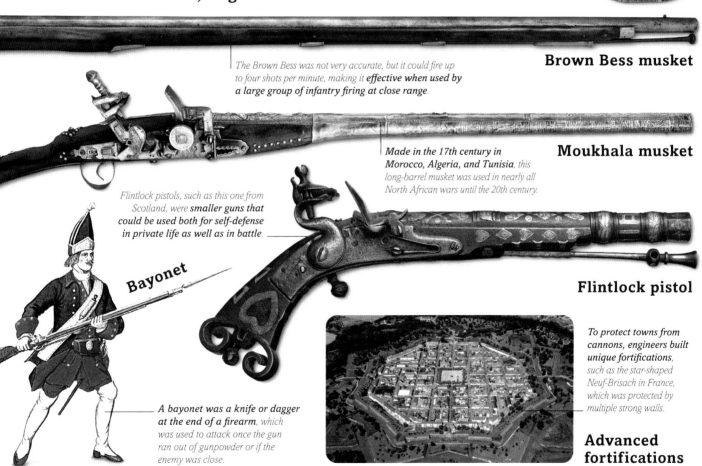

*To protect towns from cannons, engineers built **unique fortifications**, such as the star-shaped Neuf-Brisach in France, which was protected by multiple strong walls.*

Advanced fortifications

17th century many different types of guns had been developed, such as the **moukhala musket** of North Africa, the **Brown Bess musket**, which was used by both British and American soldiers during the American Revolution, and the portable **flintlock pistol**. This period was also known for its advanced sailing vessels that traveled far and wide to expand trade and empires. Warships were equipped with **demi-cannons**, which were smaller than the cannons used on battlefields but could wreck an enemy ship when fired at close range. However, advanced firepower did not always guarantee victory, as cities also began to modify and strengthen their strategies and **fortifications** to defend themselves.

European exploration

Mercator's world map

Drawn in 1569 by Flemish mapmaker Gerard Mercator, this map laid out the round Earth on a flat surface, with latitude and longitude lines spaced in a way that helped sailors navigate.

Galleon

Backstaff

Developed from an Islamic navigational tool, the mariner's astrolabe helped sailors work out the ship's distance from the Equator.

Mariner's astrolabe

The hull, or body, of the galleon was designed to store large quantities of cargo.

The backstaff allowed sailors to track their position by measuring the distance of the sun from the horizon without staring into its glare.

Padrões were **stone pillars** engraved with the Portuguese royal coat of arms.

The first padrão was set up by Portuguese explorer Diogo Cão at the mouth of the Congo River in Africa to mark his progress.

Sextant

Padrão

Caravel

The caravel had lateen (triangular) sails that made it easier to maneuver and much faster than other sailing ships.

In the 15th century, new ship designs and navigation tools allowed European sailors to undertake long voyages. At first, European explorers and traders searched for new trade routes and markets in Asia, Africa, and the Americas, but later began seizing Indigenous lands, leading to centuries of colonization.

The first voyages set off from Spain and Portugal, in search of spices and gemstones from Asia. The explorers sailed in Spanish **galleons** and Portuguese **caravels**, which could travel at great speeds and had plenty of storage for supplies and goods. Tools for nautical navigation were also developed and refined, such as the **sextant**,

French botanist Jeanne Baret, the first woman to sail around the world, in 1766–1769, had to disguise herself as a man because women were banned from ships.

Dutch East India Company

As its wealth and power grew, the Dutch East India Company *set up its own colonial government and minted its own coins, such as this one from 1735.*

Invented in 1731, the sextant *allowed sailors to accurately determine their position at sea, and this tool is still in use today.*

Jeanne Baret

In 1419, two Portuguese explorers arrived at these uninhabited islands and named them **Madeira,** *meaning "wood," after the many forested cliffsides.*

Harrison's "H1" chronometer

English clockmaker John Harrison made a series of increasingly accurate timepieces, which allowed sailors to determine how far east or west they were from a particular position.

Madeira archipelago

VOYAGES OF EXPLORATION

From the 14th–17th centuries, exploration expanded Europe's knowledge of the world. Diogo Cão was the first European to find the mouth of the Congo River; Christopher Columbus reached the Americas; and Vasco da Gama found a sea route to India. Pedro Álvares Cabral sailed to Brazil; Ferdinand Magellan's crew circumnavigated the globe; and Abel Tasman captained the first European ship to reach New Zealand.

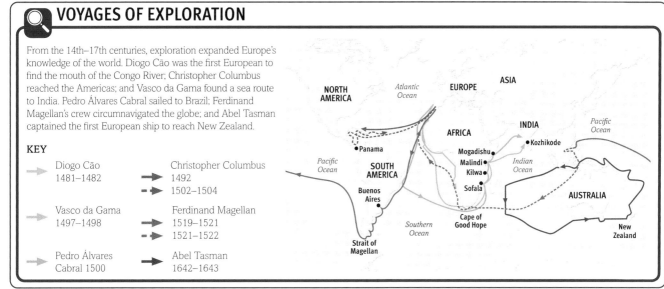

KEY

Diogo Cão
1481–1482

Vasco da Gama
1497–1498

Pedro Álvares
Cabral 1500

Christopher Columbus
1492
1502–1504

Ferdinand Magellan
1519–1521
1521–1522

Abel Tasman
1642–1643

---

backstaff, and **mariner's astrolabe**. These measured the positions of the sun and stars to help navigators work out the ship's location and the distances traveled. New maps, such as **Mercator's world map**, helped plot accurate courses. As more and more European empires began sending out ships, it led to a scramble to establish new markets as well as conquer new territories—often at the expense of Indigenous populations. Portuguese sailors left *padrões* in Africa to claim land for Portugal, while the **Dutch East India Company** established an entire city in Batavia (modern-day Jakarta in Indonesia) to control the spice trade.

The colonial Americas

At one time, at least 60 percent of the world's silver came from Potosi, a city in the Andes mountains.

Potosi silver

Foods from the Americas, such as tomatoes and potatoes, were introduced to Europe, while European, Asian, and African goods, such as sugar and onions, came to the Americas.

Columbian Exchange

Europeans brought with them deadly diseases, such as influenza, smallpox, measles, and cholera, against which the Indigenous peoples had no immunity.

Deadly epidemics

The Iglesia de la Compañia de Jesús in Cusco, Peru, is a Spanish church built on top of the palace of the Inca ruler Huayna Capac.

When the Spanish defeated the Aztec Empire, they **destroyed the old capital and built a new city, Mexico City, on top of its ruins.**

Spanish architecture

Jacques Cartier

French explorer Jacques Cartier explored the St. Lawrence River in Canada, and seized the land next to the river for France.

Destruction of Tenochtitlan

By the 17th century, Europeans had established trading ties in the Americas, but **many of their deals deceived the Indigenous peoples who lost goods and lands.**

Trading and selling

After Christopher Columbus reached the Americas in 1492, stories about the wealth found there spread across Europe. Explorers from Europe traveled to the Americas with plans of invasion or to set up colonies. This contact led to the collapse of the Indigenous civilizations that had lived there for centuries.

Europeans encountered new animals, plants, and foods in the Americas, and introduced European goods to Indigenous groups, in what became known as the **Columbian Exchange**. However, European colonizers also introduced new diseases that caused **deadly epidemics** among the local populations. The Europeans

COLONIES OF NORTH AMERICA

By 1750, the largest areas of colonization in North America had been settled by the British, Spanish, and French. They took over these territories through wars with the Indigenous people who lived there.

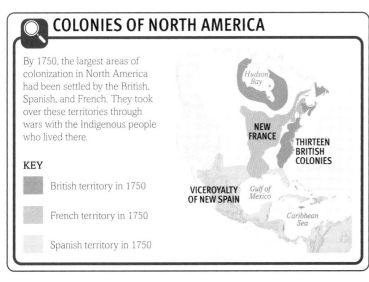

KEY

■ British territory in 1750

■ French territory in 1750

■ Spanish territory in 1750

Hudson Bay

NEW FRANCE

THIRTEEN BRITISH COLONIES

VICEROYALTY OF NEW SPAIN

Gulf of Mexico

Caribbean Sea

Trade of enslaved Africans

In 1518, King Charles V of Spain issued an order permitting the transportation of enslaved Africans to the Americas.

Although she was known as Pocahontas, the Powhatan woman's real name was **Matoaka**.

Pocahontas

Pocahontas, a translator and mediator from the Powhatan nation, was abducted by English colonists and forced to marry the settler John Rolfe.

The first English colony was set up near the James River to allow large English ships to anchor nearby.

Jamestown

The 102 passengers on the Mayflower, now known as the Pilgrims, came to North America to practice their religion freely and to find their fortunes.

The Mayflower

War in Europe between Britain and France led to conflict in the colonies from 1754–1763, with each side forging alliances with Indigenous peoples to help them in these battles.

French and Indian War

often attacked Indigenous peoples. In 1521, the Spanish, allied with some Indigenous groups, captured and **destroyed Tenochtitlan**, the capital of the Aztec Empire. In North America, the English set up their first permanent colony in 1607 at **Jamestown**. As colonies began to thrive, more Europeans came to the Americas in search of a new life, such as the passengers of the *Mayflower*. But not all new arrivals came to the Americas by choice—the **trade of enslaved Africans** (see pp.118–119) saw more than 2 million Africans forcibly transported to the Americas by the 18th century.

Drama and performance

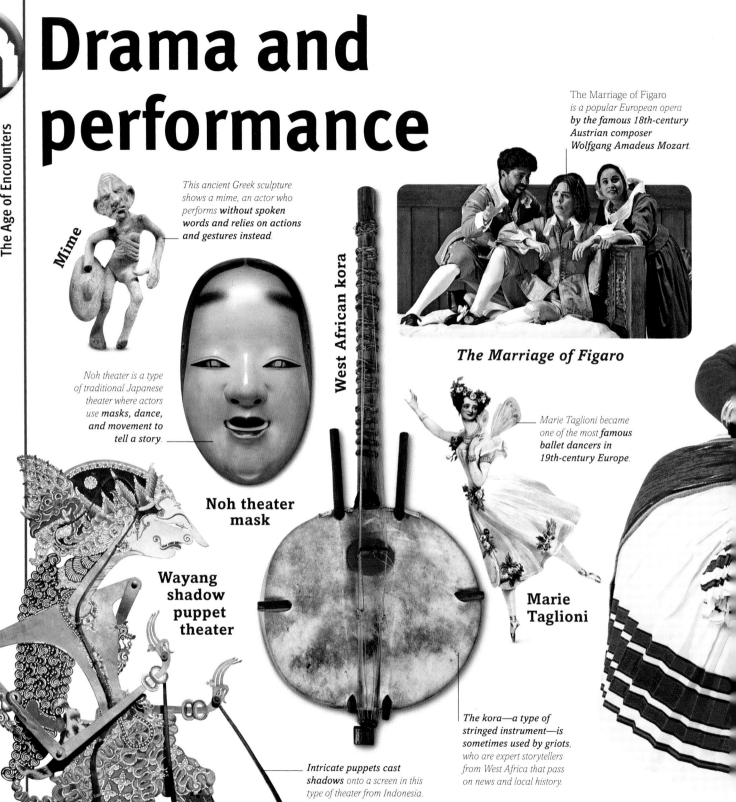

*This ancient Greek sculpture shows a mime, an actor who performs **without spoken words** and relies on actions and gestures instead.*

Mime

*The Marriage of Figaro is a popular European opera **by the famous 18th-century Austrian composer Wolfgang Amadeus Mozart**.*

The Marriage of Figaro

*Noh theater is a type of traditional Japanese theater where actors use **masks, dance, and movement to tell a story**.*

Noh theater mask

West African kora

*Marie Taglioni became one of the most **famous ballet dancers in 19th-century Europe**.*

Marie Taglioni

Wayang shadow puppet theater

*Intricate puppets cast **shadows** onto a screen in this type of theater from Indonesia.*

The kora—a type of stringed instrument—is sometimes used by griots, who are expert storytellers from West Africa that pass on news and local history.

Throughout history, people have created different forms of performance to bring joy to others, express emotions, and illustrate new perspectives on the human experience. There are many different types of performing arts around the world, including theater, movies, dance, and song.

Theater is a form of performance found in almost every culture. Among the most popular plays performed on stage today, in many countries, are those by 16th-century English playwright **William Shakespeare**. Other types of theater performance include **Wayang shadow puppet theater** and **Japanese Noh**

Kathakali dancing

Shakespearean drama

The dramatic speeches of English playwright William Shakespeare have become known all over the world.

Caribbean carnival

Every year, a variety of Caribbean islands hold vibrant **dance and music festivals** known as carnivals.

Clara Bow

Kathakali is a type of performance, originating in Kerala, India, that **combines music, singing, acting, mime, and dance.**

Clara Bow was the "it girl" of early 20th-century Hollywood and helped make movie-going popular.

The haka

Haka are Māori action dances, one of which the New Zealand national rugby team perform before every match they play.

This popular and colorful Mexican folk dance is also the national dance of the country.

Jarabe Tapatío

theater. Some performances include singing, with operas such as *The Marriage of Figaro* combining classical music with song to tell a story. Others include dance, such as **Kathakali**, which originated in India, and **ballet**, which developed in 15th-century Europe. In the early 20th century, American movie stars such as **Clara Bow** became famous around the world and helped turn movies into a popular form of performance.

The Mughal Empire

Shamshir sword

Mohur

Emperor Babur

*Babur is said to be of Mongol **descent** and was the founder of the Mughal Empire.*

*Mughal gold coins had **images of constellations**, like the Capricorn shown here, to indicate the month in which they were minted.*

The Akbarnama *was a **large** illustrated biography of the Mughal emperor Akbar.*

Painting from *Akbarnama*

🔍 THE EMPIRE'S EXTENT

Babur invaded northern India and was able to establish Mughal settlements in Delhi and Lahore. By the late 17th century, when Aurangzeb was in power, most of the Indian subcontinent had become part of the Mughal Empire.

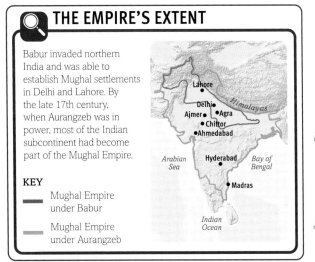

Lahore
Delhi · Agra
Ajmer · · Chittor
· Ahmedabad
Himalayas
Arabian Sea
Hyderabad
Bay of Bengal
· Madras
Indian Ocean

KEY

— Mughal Empire under Babur

— Mughal Empire under Aurangzeb

The Mughal Empire was established by the Central Asian prince Babur in 1526. Over the next 300 years, Babur's descendants ruled a large empire covering most of what is now India, Pakistan, and Bangladesh. The empire began to decline in the 18th century, but left a stunning legacy of art and architecture.

The Mughals were descendants of Central Asian Mongols, and inherited their military skills. Mughal rulers expanded their empire through multiple wars against other kingdoms, using everything from war elephants to weapons such as the **shamshir** and **khanjar** to win. As their empire grew, Mughal rulers promoted peace and

Spiked parrying shield

Mughal manuscripts contained **vibrant illustrations** and intricate calligraphy.

*Mughal soldiers may have used this **unique-looking shield** for both defense and attack on the battlefield.*

Khanjar with scabbard

This elaborate scabbard for the khanjar (dagger) is decorated with precious stones placed in floral patterns.

Mughal craft

Intricate engravings on this glass vase show the highly skilled craftwork of Mughal artisans.

*Mughal astronomers created **accurate astronomical charts** and celestial globes.*

Celestial globe

Illustrated manuscript

*Empress Nur Jahan, the wife of Emperor Jahangir, **advised her husband** on crucial matters and was an influential person in his court.*

Nur Jahan

It took more than **15 years** to build the Taj Mahal.

*The Taj Mahal was built as a **mausoleum** for Mumtaz Mahal, the wife of Emperor Shah Jahan.*

*Aurangzeb is considered to be **the last of the great Mughal rulers**, before the empire fell into decline.*

Aurangzeb

Taj Mahal

even established a common currency in the form of the gold **mohur**. Art and architecture flourished, especially under the rule of Akbar and Shah Jahan. Artists were commissioned to create beautifully **illustrated manuscripts**, such as the *Akbarnama*, which provided details of court life. The emperors also ordered the building of great cities and monuments, such as the **Taj Mahal**. In the 17th century, Emperor **Aurangzeb** brought the empire great success but, following rebellions and foreign invasions, the Mughal Empire began to crumble. In 1857, the last Mughal emperor was deposed by the British East India Company.

Qing China

Shitao was a Buddhist monk and a painter whose work was considered to be groundbreaking **because of his use of bold brushstrokes**.

Shitao's landscapes

Published in 1716, the Kangxi dictionary, **which contained more than 40,000 Chinese characters, expanded on previous dictionaries**.

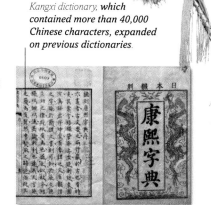

Kangxi dictionary

This palace in Beijing, **which was completed under the Qianlong Emperor in 1764**, was a summer resort for the Qing emperors.

Anger over widespread famine led to a **rebellion in 1850**, which eventually caused the death of 20–30 million people.

Summer Palace

Taiping Rebellion

In 1645, Qing prince Dorgon ordered that all men must shave the front of their head, and **wear a long braid called a queue**.

Qing artisans continued the **distinctive Chinese craft of decorating everyday objects with carved red lacquer**.

Qing porcelain

The use of five different colored glazes and firing at high temperatures gave Qing porcelain a glossy finish.

Red lacquer box

Queue

The Qing were the last dynasty of imperial China. At its height, the Qing Empire (1644–1912) ruled much of what is present-day China, Mongolia, and parts of Russia. While it became rich in the 18th century, it also began to weaken due to bad harvests, rebellions, and interference from foreign powers.

The early years of the Qing Dynasty were prosperous, and crafts flourished. Artisans produced intricate objects, such as **jade carvings** and items decorated with **red lacquer**. The ceramics industry reached new heights as the demand for high-quality **Qing porcelain** grew across Europe. The third emperor, Kangxi, was

*Developed in the late 18th and early 19th centuries, **Jingxi**, or Peking opera, involves acrobatic movements performed in elaborate costumes.*

Jingxi (Peking opera)

*While she never reigned officially in her own right, for all practical purposes, **Empress Dowager Cixi ruled the Qing Empire for 47 years.***

Empress Dowager Cixi

The boy king Puyi, known as Emperor Xuantong, had to give up his throne when the Xinhai Revolution ended imperial China.

*In 1899, a group of martial artists began the Boxer Rebellion **against the growing dominance of Britain and Japan in China.***

Boxer Rebellion

Emperor Puyi

*In Chinese culture, jade is associated **with purity** and is often carved into luxury and religious items.*

Qing jade carving

a supporter of literature and commissioned many books, including the **Kangxi dictionary**. In the mid-19th century, *Jingxi* (**Peking opera**) became a popular way of telling historical and cultural stories. However, the empire began to decline after the **Taiping Rebellion**, which became a civil war. A series of natural disasters and famines also assisted Qing decline. Imperial power was further weakened by the failed **Boxer Rebellion** against foreign powers. The last Qing emperor, **Puyi**, was crowned at the age of two, but reigned for only four years before the Xinhai Revolution ended Qing rule in 1912 and made China a republic.

Edo Japan

Tokugawa Ieyasu

The son of a Japanese feudal lord, Ieyasu fought more than 90 battles before unifying Japan.

Sumo wrestlers wore a belt-like garment called **mawashi**, *which could be grabbed when lifting opponents out of the ring.*

Sumo wrestling

The brightly colored makeup on a kabuki actor's face is called **kumadori** *and lets viewers know the character's social class and personality.*

Kabuki

Jitte

This weapon, made using steel and silk, became popular after swords were banned across the country.

One of the most famous poets of this period, **Matsuo Bashō** *helped develop a short form of poetry with just three phrases, known as a haiku.*

A bunraku puppet could be up to 4 ft (1.2 m) tall and had to be operated by three people.

Geisha

Matsuo Bashō

Bunraku puppet

Geishas were highly skilled in many forms of entertainment, from playing instruments to calligraphy.

A kabuki actor's costume could **weigh** more than **66 lb (30 kg)**.

After centuries of bitter battles, Japan was united in 1603 under the Tokugawa Shogunate. The town of Edo, now modern-day Tokyo, became the center of the shogun's power until the late 19th century. The stability of Edo Japan allowed culture to flourish, giving rise to new forms of poetry, art, and theater.

In 1600, shogun **Tokugawa Ieyasu** won a major victory at the Battle of Sekigahara (see pp.78–79), ending years of constant fighting. This led to great cultural and social activity. City life thrived as people flocked to **sumo wrestling** matches, while **kabuki** theaters entertained patrons with shows. Women were banned from acting, but could train as **geishas**,

Travel within Japan

The Tōkaidō Road, one of the five major highways that connected Edo to the rest of Japan, became a popular route for travelers during the Edo period.

Ukiyo-e painting

Ukiyo-e, meaning "pictures of the floating world," gets its name from Edo's pleasure district, which was often the subject of these paintings.

Carved from ivory or wood, netsuke were worn by men on their sashes, and worked as toggles or buttons.

Netsuke

Woodblock printing

Japanese woodblock printing involves chiseling an image on a wooden block, inking it, and then pressing it on paper.

Imari ware

Painstaking detail and a rich color palette made Edo porcelain ware popular items for export.

Emperor Meiji was restored to the throne at the age of 15 and ruled for 45 years.

Meiji Restoration

learning how to sing, dance, play instruments, and perform tea ceremonies to entertain people. A style of painting called **ukiyo-e** flourished during this period, depicting the lives of the common people. However, this era of peace was achieved by Japan isolating itself from the rest of the world—a policy called *sakoku*. Foreign trade was limited and very few people were allowed in or out of the country. Tokugawa Iesada opened Japan's borders in 1854, increasing opposition to the shogunate. In 1868, the last Tokugawa shogun was overthrown, and political power was restored to the monarchy in the **Meiji Restoration**.

The Atlantic slave trade

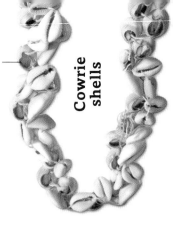

These small shells were a form of currency in Africa, and many African people were sold by local merchants or military leaders to European traders in exchange for them.

Cowrie shells

Cape Coast Castle

European slave traders imprisoned enslaved people along the coast of West Africa in forts such as this one, before shipping them to the colonies.

Brookes ship

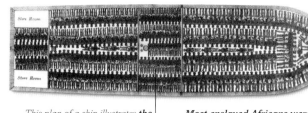

This plan of a ship illustrates the inhumanely constricted conditions enslaved people had to endure below deck on their journey across the Atlantic Ocean.

Most enslaved Africans were forced to labor 18 hours a day on cotton and sugar plantations in the Americas and the Caribbean.

Queen Nzinga

In 1619, a group of 20 enslaved Africans were sold to settlers in the colony of Virginia, beginning slavery in what would become the US.

Enslaved people in Virginia

Queen Nzinga was a ruler in modern-day Angola who fought against Portuguese slave traders.

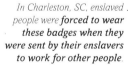

In Charleston, SC, enslaved people were forced to wear these badges when they were sent by their enslavers to work for other people.

Charleston badge

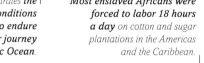

In one of the most horrific episodes in human history, between the 16th and 19th centuries more than 12 million Africans were forcibly taken from their communities, enslaved, and transported to the Americas and the Caribbean. Those who survived the journey were sold into a miserable lifetime of hard labor.

European traders purchased enslaved Africans from the interior regions of the African continent in exchange for **cowrie shells**, alcohol, and weaponry. The enslaved people were brought to forts such as **Cape Coast Castle**, before being shipped to colonies in the Americas and the Caribbean in cramped ships like the *Brookes*. This journey could take from one to

Auctioning the enslaved

Auction houses displayed enslaved people like property or objects for sale, and even subjected them to being examined by buyers.

Harriet Tubman

Harriet Tubman, a formerly enslaved woman, helped hundreds of people escape slavery in the Southern states of the US.

Enslaved Africans were often violently abused by their enslavers, using tools such as this field whip.

Field whip

Toussaint L'Ouverture successfully led an army of enslaved African people to put an end to French control of Haiti.

Toussaint L'Ouverture

This medallion with the inscription "Am I not a man and a brother?" became an important symbol of the anti-slavery movements in Britain and the US.

Abolitionist movement

Working on plantations

🔍 JUNETEENTH CELEBRATIONS

Slavery was abolished in the United States in 1863 when President Abraham Lincoln issued the Emancipation Proclamation. However, it took until June 19, 1865, for this news to reach people in Texas. Today, June 19, called Juneteenth, is a federal holiday in the US.

---

three months, and many Africans died on the way due to diseases or brutal treatment by the ship's crew. Once in the colonies, enslaved Africans were sold at **auctions** and then forced to work on large farms called **plantations**. Life on plantations involved long working hours, the constant threat of beatings, and very little food or rest. Many enslaved people rebelled against plantation owners, or ran away to escape slavery. By the mid-19th century, anti-slavery movements were growing. This was due to the efforts of formerly enslaved people, such as **Harriet Tubman**, and global **abolitionist movements**. They led to the abolition of slavery in the Americas by the end of the 19th century.

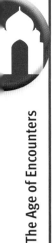
African kingdoms

Sword of the Sultan of Darfur

Crucifix from Kongo

This sword belonged to the last Sultan of Darfur, a powerful kingdom in what is present-day Sudan.

Many people in the Kingdom of Kongo converted to Roman Catholicism after encountering Portuguese traders in the 15th century.

Merina sculpture

The Kingdom of Merina, on the island of Madagascar, produced many beautifully carved wooden sculptures.

The **Benin Bronzes** were **looted** by British soldiers in **1897**.

This statue of King Béhanzin of Dahomey was stolen by invading French soldiers in 1892.

These sculptures were commissioned by the royal court to commemorate past rulers of the Kingdom of Benin.

Dahomey statue

The all-female army called the Mino *were* **known as the "Dahomey Amazons"** *by Europeans.*

Mino

In the 15th to 18th centuries, the wealth of Africa saw new kingdoms arise. Local trade routes grew across the continent, and some kingdoms began dealing with Europe in goods and enslaved people. This period produced some of the finest examples of African art, such as the Benin Bronzes.

Increased trade with Europe not only brought goods to Africa, but new religion, too. Portuguese traders introduced Roman Catholicism to the Kingdom of Kongo in Central Africa, and local artists began producing Christian art, such as **crucifixes**. Founded in the 13th century, the Kingdom of Benin (in present-day Nigeria) was

Benin Bronzes

Among the great African kingdoms that flourished between 1450 and 1750 were the kingdoms of Benin, Songhai, and Kanem-Bornu in West Africa. Farther south, in Central Africa, was the Kingdom of Kongo. To the east, in what is now Sudan, lay the Sultanate of Darfur.

KEY

- Kanem-Bornu
- Kingdom of Kongo
- Songhai Empire
- Benin Empire
- Sultanate of Darfur

SONGHAI EMPIRE
KANEM-BORNU
Red Sea
SULTANATE OF DARFUR
BENIN EMPIRE
Atlantic Ocean
KINGDOM OF KONGO

The Akan people, from modern-day Ghana and Ivory Coast, created **intricate terra-cotta heads in the 17th and 18th centuries.**

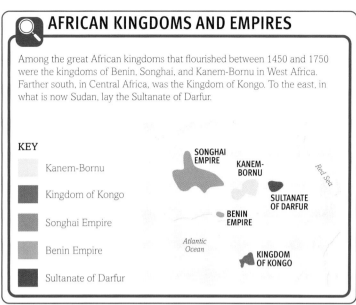

Mounted warriors were tasked with defending Kanem-Bornu, a large empire in Central and North Africa.

Kanem-Bornu warriors

Akan terra-cotta

Askia was the second emperor of Songhai, a large trading empire in what is present-day Mali, Niger, and Nigeria.

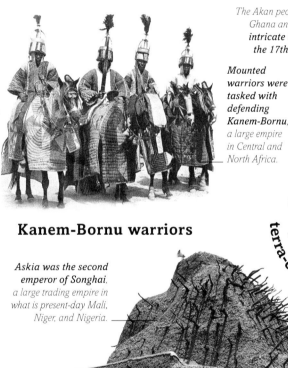

Udamalore

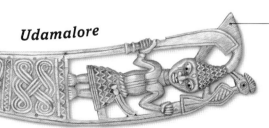

A high-ranking chief in Owo, a Yoruba state in what is now Nigeria, carried this sword.

Tomb of Askia

home to elaborate architecture, such as the royal palace, the original home of the **Benin Bronzes**. The Kingdom of Benin traded with ivory workers from the city-state of Owo to the north, whose chief carried an ivory **udamalore** ("sword of the well-born"). In what is today Ghana and the Ivory Coast, the Akan people made beautiful **terra-cotta heads**. These were created by female elders to remember the dead. West Africa was also home to the Kingdom of Dahomey, which had an all-female army, known as the ***Mino***, who defended the kingdom until it became a French colony in the late 19th century.

THE AGE OF REVOLUTION

The Age of Revolution

From the late 18th century, a series of revolutions rocked the world. Colonies fought for independence, regions revolted against harsh rulers, Indigenous and enslaved people rose up against oppression, and unrest spread in Europe.

The period from the late 18th to the early 20th centuries saw uprisings and revolutions break out in Europe and its colonies. Most of the colonies in North and South America won their independence, while a revolution in France saw the end of its monarchy. This period, however, was also the high point of European colonial power, with European empires stretching their rule across much of Africa, Asia, and Oceania.

The Industrial Revolution

Not every revolution during this period was a political struggle. In 18th-century Britain, a technological revolution began that would change the way people lived and worked around the world. The Industrial Revolution created new jobs in factories, resulting in a massive shift in population from rural areas to towns and cities. Transportation underwent great changes, with the expansion of canal networks and the construction of railroads.

MEIJI MODERNIZATION
The Industrial Revolution in Japan took place during the Meiji Restoration, a time of modernization that occurred between 1868 and 1912, later than the period of industrialization in Europe and the US. During the Meiji Restoration, Japan constructed railroads, set up a telegraph network, and created a new education system.

Though it originated in Britain, the Industrial Revolution soon spread across much of Europe and the US, and to other parts of the world in the 19th and early 20th centuries.

Rejecting authority

Independence movements in the Americas saw their first success when Britain's thirteen colonies broke away from colonial rule and formed the United States of America. They claimed independence in 1776, and became the first independent country in the Americas after victory in the American Revolution (1775–1783) ended British rule. Over the next fifty years, Spanish and Portuguese colonial rule came to an end in Mexico and much of South America as liberation movements spread throughout the region.

THE RIDE OF PAUL REVERE
American silversmith Paul Revere is best known for his "midnight ride" on April 18, 1775, to warn colonial forces of the arrival of British troops on the eve of the first battles of the American Revolution at Lexington and Concord.

Inspired by the example set by the American Revolution, starving French peasants took to the streets to rebel against the French monarchy. The French Revolution would eventually lead to the execution of King Louis XVI in 1793 and the establishment of a French government run by the people. Elsewhere in Europe, Serbia and Greece fought for independence from the Ottoman Empire. In 1848, a series of revolutions swept across Europe, calling for reforms that would eventually lead to greater equality and democracy.

REVOLUTIONARY COCKADE

The early French Revolutionary Army wore bicorn (two-cornered) hats with a tricolor cockade (badge) in red, white, and blue, representing the colors of the monarchy and the city of Paris.

Colonial control and resistance

As European colonial powers continued to expand their territory and exert control over faraway lands, Indigenous and enslaved people who lived there often fought back against colonial rule. They were not always successful—the Indians rebelled against British rule on many occasions, but the British continued to rule over the Indian subcontinent until after World War II.

DELHI DURBAR

The British Empire marked the succession of a new Emperor or Empress of India with a Delhi Durbar ("Court of Delhi"). This mass assembly was held three times at Coronation Park in Delhi.

TREATY OF WAITANGI

In 1840, about 540 Māori Rangatira (chiefs) signed the Treaty of Waitangi. The treaty gave Britain the right to buy Māori lands in exchange for defending them from other colonizing powers. However, arguments over the treaty's exact meaning led to future conflicts, and settlers at times ignored its terms to claim new lands.

Sometimes powers entered into treaties with Indigenous peoples and made promises that they later ignored. This was the case with the Treaty of Waitangi between Britain and Māori chiefs of New Zealand. The US also went back on treaties that it had signed with Indigenous peoples as it expanded westward.

Some rebellions were successful. In Haiti in the Caribbean, enslaved people rose up against French rule. The Haitian Revolution ended French control of Haiti, which became an independent country in 1804. In Africa, various European empires claimed territory across the continent in the late 19th century, but the people of Ethiopia defeated an invading Italian army at the Battle of Adwa in 1896, ending Italian plans to start an empire in Africa.

The Industrial Revolution

The flying shuttle got its name from its ability to weave fabric at a faster rate than ever before.

Kay's flying shuttle

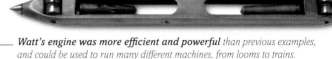

This steam engine was mostly used to pump water out of coal mines, a job that was previously done by horses pulling buckets on a rope.

Newcomen's steam engine

Watt's engine was more efficient and powerful than previous examples, and could be used to run many different machines, from looms to trains.

German engineer Gottlieb Daimler developed a combustion engine that could run on gasoline, and attached it to a bicycle to create the first motorcycle.

Daimler's combustion engine

Watt's steam engine

British industrialist Richard Arkwright opened the first modern factory, a cotton spinning mill, in Cromford, UK.

Arkwright's factory

British inventor Samuel Crompton's machine combined weaving and spinning into one, allowing a single person to work more than 1,000 spindles at the same time.

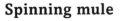

Spinning mule

The Industrial Revolution began in Britain in the 18th century as a series of inventions changed the way people lived and worked. Many moved from farms to live in towns and work in factories. European nations and the US soon began to industrialize, making further technological advancements.

The first steam engine was invented in Britain by **Thomas Newcomen** in the 1700s. By the 1760s, **James Watt** had built an improved version that revolutionized production—powering flour, paper, and cotton mills; ironworks; waterworks; and canals. New British inventions, such as the **flying shuttle** and the **spinning mule**, increased

Whitney's cotton gin

A single gin could clean up to 50 lb (23 kg) of cotton a day.

Trevithick's locomotive

British inventor Richard Trevithick built this steam-powered locomotive in 1804.

George Stephenson's Locomotion No. 1 was the train engine that pulled the world's first public train.

Locomotion No. 1

In 1831, a group of hand tailors attacked and **destroyed** all of Thimonnier's machines.

The diesel engine became popular for being more efficient and cheaper than coal, which saved transportation companies money.

Diesel engine

Barthélemy Thimonnier patented the first mass-produced sewing machine in France in 1830.

Thimonnier's sewing machine

Scottish-born Alexander Graham Bell moved to the US to work as a teacher for the deaf, and invented the telephone in 1876.

Telephone

US inventors Samuel Morse and Alfred Vail built the electric telegraph and devised a code consisting of dots and dashes to send messages.

Telegraph

productivity, leading to factories full of workers making goods that had global demand. By the late 19th century, inventions in other countries, such as Germany and the US, changed the world even further. German engineer Rudolf Diesel created the **diesel engine**, which transformed the transportation industry by reducing the need for coal. In the Southern US, the invention of the **cotton gin** made separating seeds from cotton fiber faster, boosting cotton production and the demand for enslaved labor to pick cotton. Long distance communication became possible with the invention of the **telephone** and **telegraph**.

Independence in the Americas

George Washington led the Continental Army to victory over the British and later helped draft the US Constitution.

George Washington

This coat is part of the uniform of the military force set up by the colonies in 1775, which fought against the British during the American Revolution.

On July 4, 1776, the US Continental Congress issued the Declaration of Independence, and this date is now celebrated as Independence Day.

Declaration of Independence

Liberty Bell

The once widely believed story that the first US flag was designed by American seamstress Elizabeth "Betsy" Ross was spread by her family.

The Liberty Bell in Philadelphia, PA, was rung on July 8, 1776, to call people to hear the first public reading of the Declaration of Independence.

Betsy Ross flag

Continental Army coat

By the 18th century, colonies in the Americas had developed to the point of wishing to govern themselves, and felt that the European empires should no longer control or exploit them. Independence movements began, turning the continents into battlegrounds as revolutionaries led the fight for freedom.

Conflict began in North America when the Thirteen Colonies began resisting the taxes imposed on them by the British Empire. This triggered the American Revolution in 1775. The Continental Army was led by General **George Washington**, who would later become the first US president. In 1776, the new nation of the United States of America announced

The Battle of Suipacha in 1810 saw the first defeat of the Spanish colonial army *during the war of independence for Upper Peru (modern-day Bolivia).*

Battle of Suipacha

Battle of Maipú

This battle in 1818 saw South American forces under Argentine general José de San Martín defeat the Spanish army, leading to the **liberation of Chile and Peru**.

Religious banners showing the Virgin Mary were waved by followers of **Mexican priest Miguel Hidalgo**, who gave a speech that triggered the Mexican Revolution.

Mexican Revolution

Gran Colombia flag

In 1821, this flag represented Gran Colombia, *or the Republic of Colombia—a vast area including modern-day Colombia, Ecuador, Panama, and Venezuela.*

Argentine revolutionary **Manuel Belgrano** *fought for his country's freedom and also created Argentina's flag.*

Manuel Belgrano

José Antonio Páez fought for **Venezuela's independence**, *first from Spain and later from Gran Colombia.*

José Antonio Páez

Known as "the Liberator," Dom Pedro I was the founder of the **Empire of Brazil** *after declaring the nation independent from Portugal in 1822.*

Dom Pedro I

Simón Bolívar

Spanish cavalry pistol

New firearms with swift-shooting mechanisms *were used by the Spanish cavalry in many colonial conflicts.*

Venezuelan general Simón Bolívar fought across South America *and was instrumental in the independence of six nations: Colombia, Venezuela, Ecuador, Peru, Panama, and Bolivia.*

its freedom from British rule with the **Declaration of Independence**, becoming the first free country in the Americas. Other places also saw revolutions, such as Haiti in 1804 (see pp.138–139) and Mexico. The **Mexican Revolution** of 1810 lasted a decade before Spanish colonial rule ended and an independent Mexico was born. By 1825, Spanish and Portuguese rule over much of South America had ended. This was due to the actions of leaders like **Dom Pedro I** of Brazil, **Manuel Belgrano** and José de San Martín of Argentina, and **Simón Bolívar** of Venezuela, who ultimately brought lasting independence across the Americas.

Building and dividing America

Settlers moving westward packed all their belongings in horse-drawn, canvas-covered *wagons*, and traveled in groups for safety on the long journey.

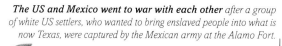
The US and Mexico went to war with each other after a group of white US settlers, who wanted to bring enslaved people into what is now Texas, were captured by the Mexican army at the Alamo Fort.

*A skilled translator from the Shoshone nation, Sacagawea guided explorers **Lewis and Clark** across Indigenous areas, helping them communicate with the peoples living there.*

War with Mexico

Covered wagon

Sacagawea

Gold was found in California in early 1848, leading to an influx of people from across the country hoping to make a fortune.

California gold rush

The Homestead Act of 1862 granted land in the western United States to settlers who agreed to live on and improve the land for five years.

Homestead Act

Around **179,000** Black soldiers served in the Union Army during the Civil War.

After the American Revolution (1775–1783), the new nation began increasing the territory under its control. Large swathes of land were stolen from Indigenous nations or bought from other colonial powers. The country was also plunged into a civil war over the enslavement of Black people.

The US bought the district of Louisiana from the French Empire in 1803, and in 1804, Lemhi Shoshone guide **Sacagawea** helped Meriwether Lewis and William Clark explore this region. In 1848, the US gained the territory of Texas after a long period of **war with Mexico**. The addition of new lands, and the discovery of **gold in California**,

Civil War battle drum

President Lincoln gave a now-famous speech on fighting for equality after the Battle of Gettysburg during the Civil War.

*Drums were used by soldiers **to keep the beat** on marches or to signal instructions on the battlefield.*

Abraham Lincoln

Many women, such as nurse Dorothea Dix, provided medical care to wounded soldiers during the Civil War.

Dorothea Dix

After slavery was abolished in 1863, a large number of Black men joined the Union Army to fight in the Civil War.

*Uniforms worn by Confederate soldiers were simple, homemade outfits, while **Confederate** officers wore embellished gray coats such as this one.*

Confederate uniform

Completed during the Reconstruction period in 1869, this railroad connected the eastern and western regions of the US.

Transcontinental railroad

4th US Colored Infantry

*In 1870, the US government gave some **Black men the right to vote**, but many southern states still resisted this change.*

Reconstruction

prompted settlers to move westward, traveling in **covered wagons**. However, these lands belonged to Indigenous peoples, who fought many bloody wars with the United States to protect their territories (see pp. 132–133). In 1858, the election of the anti-slavery president **Abraham Lincoln** caused division in the country. A civil war broke

out in 1861 between the Union (northern states), which wanted to limit slavery, and the Confederacy (southern states), which did not. The war ended with a Union victory in 1865, and was followed by a **Reconstruction** period where laws were passed that were supposed to give more rights to Black people.

Indigenous peoples and the United States

Henry repeating rifle

This rifle could fire up to 15 shots without needing to be reloaded and was used by both US soldiers and Indigenous fighters.

Tomahawk

*A type of ax, the tomahawk was a **deadly handheld weapon** that could also be thrown at an enemy.*

A strong military leader, Chief Ma-ka-tai-me-she-kia-kia (Black Hawk) is said to have led successful raids and war parties when he was just a teenager.

Chief Tecumseh

To protect his lands from white settlers, Chief Tecumseh allied with the British against the US in the War of 1812.

Ma-ka-tai-me-she-kia-kia

In 1864, US troops attacked a peaceful camp of the Tsis tsis'tas (Cheyenne) and Hinono-eino (Arapaho), killing 230 people, including 150 women, children, and old people.

The Sand Creek Massacre

The Trail of Tears

In the late 18th century, the US began to expand its borders into more lands that belonged to Indigenous groups. Some fought back, while others entered into treaties with the new nation. When the US began ignoring these treaties, the stage was set for more brutal conflicts with the Indigenous peoples.

Among the many Indigenous leaders who fought against US encroachment was **Chief Tecumseh**, leader of the Shawnee, who pushed for intertribal unity to resist the US forces. The Sauk and Meskwaki nations under Chief **Ma-ka-tai-me-she-kia-kia** (Black Hawk) also fought, but failed, to reclaim the land that had been taken from them.

Battle of the Greasy Grass

This statue was built at the site of the Battle of the Greasy Grass in memory of the Indigenous warriors who died defending their lands and way of life.

Goyathlay

Leader of the Lakota Nation, Chief Tatanka Iyotake (Sitting Bull) made a peace treaty with the US, before leading the Lakota to war when the US abandoned the treaty.

In 1890, up to 300 Lakota people were massacred when the US Army tried to stop them from performing a religious dance.

Tatanka Iyotake

Wounded Knee Massacre

From 1830 to 1850, more than 100,000 Indigenous people were forced to relocate west, and this difficult journey killed more than 15,000.

A leader of the Bedonkohe Apache people, Goyathlay (Geronimo) led raids on US settlements from his mountain hideouts.

🔍 INDIGENOUS LANDS

Believing that it was the destiny of the United States to expand westward, Americans quickly moved toward the Pacific coast. US wars for land drastically reduced the Indigenous populations, and by 1890, most of the original inhabitants of North America had been forced to live on reservations.

KEY

— Indigenous territory, 1850

Pacific Ocean

— Reservations, 1890

Indigenous peoples and the United States

In 1830, US president Andrew Jackson signed the Indian Removal Act, and the Muscogee (Creek), Seminole, Chickasaw, and Ani-yun-wiya (Cherokee) people were forced to leave their homes and travel to "Indian territories" hundreds of miles away. This journey cost many lives, and came to be called **the Trail of Tears**. When the US abandoned its treaty with the Lakota Nation, it led to the Black Hills War of 1876, in which Chief **Tatanka Iyotake** (Sitting Bull) defeated US forces at the **Battle of the Greasy Grass**. Today, many Indigenous peoples live in limited areas called "reservations" and are fighting to reclaim access to their ancestral lands.

European revolutions

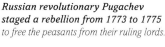

Russian revolutionary Pugachev staged a rebellion from 1773 to 1775 to free the peasants from their ruling lords.

Yemelyan Pugachev

*Leading the Society of United Irishmen, **Wolfe Tone fought to end English rule in Ireland in the 18th century.***

Around 600 protesters broke into the Bastille prison in Paris in 1789 and freed the prisoners, igniting the French Revolution.

Storming of the Bastille

Wolfe Tone

*A gathering of 10,000 protesters from rural parts of Zurich in 1830 **led to a new Swiss constitution the following year.***

This statue commemorates Prince Miloš Obrenović, who led two national uprisings in Serbia during the Serbian Revolution.

Ustertag Switzerland

Serbian Revolution

French Revolution of 1848

The throne was burned where the **Bastille prison** once stood.

The throne of King Louis Philippe was burned by revolutionaries protesting against economic inequality during the French Revolution of 1848.

Between the end of the 18th century and the middle of the 19th century, Europe became the scene of political and social unrest, leading to revolutions in many countries. One of the driving forces behind many of these revolutions was the demand of the people for more democratic and equal societies.

The French Revolution of 1789 started with the **storming of the Bastille** prison and ended with the nation becoming a republic (see pp.136–137). This successful uprising inspired revolutionaries across Europe, such as **Wolfe Tone**, who fought to free Ireland from English rule. Both Serbia and Greece, which were ruled by the Ottoman Empire,

Frankfurt Parliament

The Frankfurt Parliament was established at St. Paul's Church in 1848 in response to calls for German unification and a new constitution.

Hungarian cockade

Giuseppe Garibaldi

Naval commander Bouboulina captained the **Agamemnon**, *the largest ship of the Greek Navy during the Greek War of Independence.*

Cockades in the three colors of the Hungarian flag are worn on March 15 to commemorate the start of the Hungarian Revolution of 1848.

Italian general Giuseppe Garibaldi fought to unify Italy, finally succeeding in 1861.

In 1867, members of the Irish Republican Brotherhood, also known as **Fenians,** *attacked an English prison van to release Irish prisoners.*

Fenian Rising

Laskarina Bouboulina

🔍 REVOLUTIONARY NEWSPAPER

At the same time as the French Revolution of 1848, French writer Eugénie Mouchon-Niboyet was fighting for women's rights to equality. From 1848 to 1852, she published *La Voix des Femmes* ("The Voice of Women"), the nation's first newspaper that advocated progress, equality, and opportunities for women, including the right to vote and to be elected.

Eugénie Mouchon-Niboyet

saw their people rise up. Miloš Obrenović fought in the **Serbian Revolution** (1804–1835), and **Laskarina Bouboulina** played an important role in the Greek War of Independence (1821–1829). It was in 1848, however, that a wave of revolutions swept across Europe. In France, which had again become a monarchy, the **French Revolution of** **1848** brought about a second republic. In Germany, the **Frankfurt Parliament** was established to unify the country, while in Hungary, people forced the government to bring in reforms, such as abolishing serfdom (forced peasant labor), proving that revolutions could bring about significant change.

THE FRENCH REVOLUTION

In the late 18th century, as the gap between rich and poor widened, France became the scene of riots and revolution. Thousands of peasants, including women and children, took to the streets rebelling against the leadership of King Louis XVI and the ruling classes. Their actions eventually brought an end to centuries of royal rule in France.

The French Revolution began in June 1789, when a mob stormed the Bastille prison in Paris and set free seven political prisoners. By October, serious food shortages prompted 7,000 armed women to march toward the Palace of Versailles, demanding bread for their children. Radical revolutionaries called for "Liberty, Equality, Fraternity!"—which became the slogan of the revolution. King Louis XVI and Queen Marie Antoinette were captured and the monarchy was abolished and replaced by a government run by the people. However, the new government was unstable and executed thousands of people, including the king and queen, to maintain its control.

Resistance to colonialism

Enslaved Mexican Gaspar Yanga led a revolt in 1570 against the Spanish and then hid in the forest, establishing his own free colony.

Gaspar Yanga

Taking his name from the last Inca emperor, Túpac Amaru II led a rebellion against Spanish rule in Peru.

Túpac Amaru II

An enslaved Jamaican preacher, Samuel Sharpe led a strike to protest against working conditions on the plantations, which turned into a full rebellion in 1831.

Samuel Sharpe

Born into slavery, Dessalines rose to become one of the leaders of the Haitian Revolution against French rule.

Dessalines became **Emperor Jacques I** of Haiti in **1804**.

Jean-Jacques Dessalines

Tipu Sultan, also known as the "Tiger of Mysore," owned this organ shaped like a tiger mauling a British soldier.

Tipu Sultan's tiger organ

As European powers established empires around the world, many local people resisted foreign rule. There were examples of resistance against all the empires, but while some were successful in ending colonial rule, others paid a terrible price for their rebellion.

Indians resisted British rule on many occasions. **Tipu Sultan** fought four wars against the British between 1767 and 1799, finally falling on the battlefield after being betrayed. In Peru, decades before a successful series of independence movements swept across South America, a rebellion broke out against Spanish rule in 1780.

From 1845 to 1872, a series of wars broke out between the British colonial government and Māori people opposing the British takeover of their lands.

The New Zealand Wars

Lakshmi Bai, the Maharani (queen) of Jhansi, was one of the leaders of the Indian Rebellion in 1857, which was crushed by British forces.

Rani of Jhansi

The Tagalog War

The Filipino people launched a revolt against the Spanish in 1896 after more than three centuries of colonial rule.

Inspired by a religious leader known as the Mahdi, in 1881–1899 the people of Sudan fought a war against Egypt, and later Britain, which ended with British rule over Sudan.

COLONIAL RESPONSE

In 1904, the Herero and Nama people of Namibia rebelled against German colonial rule. The Germans responded by ordering the extermination of the Indigenous people. About 80,000 were killed in what is considered to be the first genocide of the 20th century.

In 1896, Ethiopian forces defeated an invading Italian army, halting Italian attempts to build an empire in Africa.

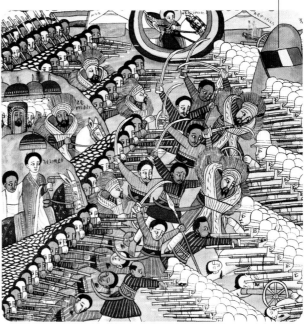

The Battle of Adwa

The Mahdist War

It was led by **Túpac Amaru II**, who was executed by the Spanish. In many colonies, enslaved people also rebelled against the colonizers. A revolution broke out in 1791 in the Caribbean, as enslaved people in Haiti rose up against French rule. In 1804, Haiti became an independent country under the rule of General **Jean-Jacques Dessalines**. In Jamaica, another Caribbean island, the Baptist War of 1831–1832 saw about 60,000 enslaved people join a strike, which turned into an unsuccessful rebellion against British rule. Its leader, **Samuel Sharpe**, was hanged for his defiance. Britain abolished slavery in its colonies just one year later.

Advances in medicine

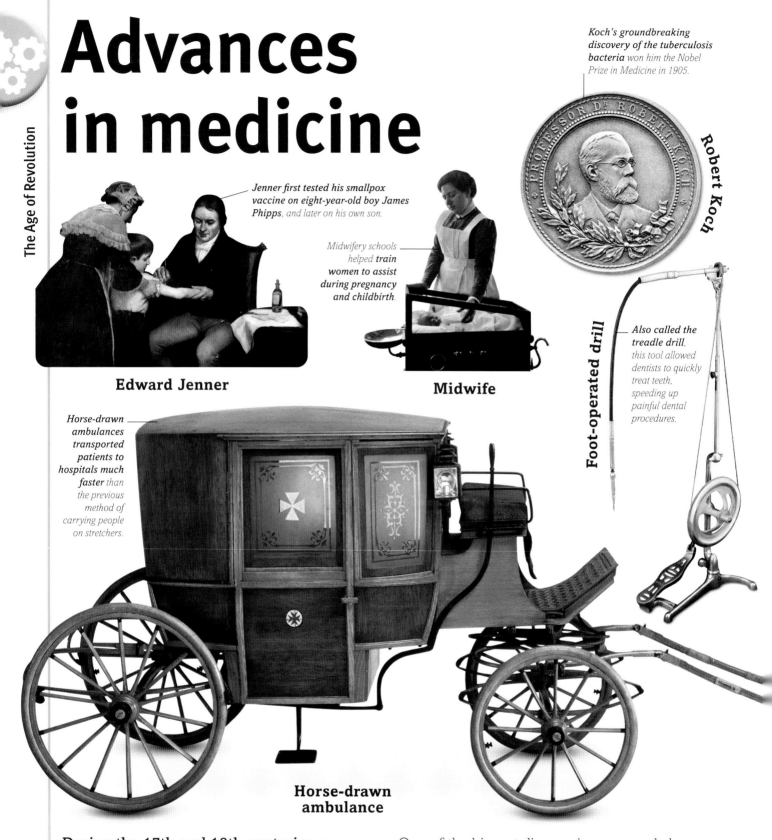

Koch's groundbreaking discovery of the tuberculosis bacteria won him the Nobel Prize in Medicine in 1905.

Robert Koch

Jenner first tested his smallpox vaccine on eight-year-old boy James Phipps, and later on his own son.

Edward Jenner

Midwifery schools helped train women to assist during pregnancy and childbirth.

Midwife

Foot-operated drill

Also called the treadle drill, this tool allowed dentists to quickly treat teeth, speeding up painful dental procedures.

Horse-drawn ambulances transported patients to hospitals much faster than the previous method of carrying people on stretchers.

Horse-drawn ambulance

During the 17th and 18th centuries, a scientific approach to health care steadily replaced religion-based thinking. In new hospitals funded by rich patrons, trained physicians could explore why illnesses occurred while treating patients' symptoms free of charge, and try to find cures.

One of the biggest discoveries was made by British doctor **Edward Jenner** who, in 1796, proved the effectiveness of vaccines. Nearly 90 years later, French chemist **Louis Pasteur** created a vaccine to both treat and prevent the deadly rabies infection. Advancements were also made in emergency medicine, where

Skilled battlefield surgeons could perform amputations **within minutes**.

Using tools to amputate injured limbs helped prevent infection from spreading to the body, and saved lives in the American Civil War (1861–1865).

Field surgery tools

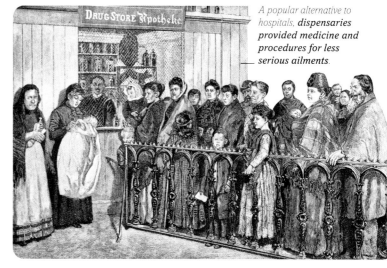

*A popular alternative to hospitals, **dispensaries** provided medicine and procedures for less serious ailments.*

Dispensaries

Morton's ether inhaler

French doctor René Laënnec's wooden stethoscope allowed doctors to listen to a patient's chest from a hygienic distance.

Stethoscope

Lister and antiseptics

*The anesthetic placed inside a Morton's ether inhaler helped **put patients to sleep before painful procedures**.*

British surgeon Joesph Lister was the first to use carbolic acid as an antiseptic in his operating room.

Florence Nightingale

*This bronze bust was funded by British Army soldiers to **acknowledge Nightingale's services** during the Crimean War.*

PIONEERING WOMEN

As medical science moved forward, a handful of women defied the norms and prejudices of their day to study medicine. Three in particular—India's Anandibai Joshi, Japan's Kei Okami, and Syria's Tabat M. Islambooly—were each the first woman in their country to gain a degree in Western medicine.

Kei Okami

Anandibai Joshi

Tabat M. Islambooly

As well as creating a rabies vaccine, Pasteur also discovered that germs cause diseases.

Louis Pasteur

gruesome-looking **field surgery tools** were used during wars for life-saving procedures. Other pioneering instruments allowed for improved practices—including the first **stethoscope**, and the **foot-operated drill** for dentists. While doctors and surgeons were usually male, nursing duties fell to women. The most famous nurse was perhaps **Florence Nightingale**, who cared for soldiers in the Crimean War (1853–1856). **Midwives** played an important part in how childbirth was managed in hospitals. Trained midwives meant good health care could now start at the very beginning of life.

141

Travel and transportation

An enormous front wheel enabled the rider to reach high speeds by pedaling.

Penny Farthing

This transatlantic steamship became the first passenger ship to cross the Atlantic in just 14 days.

A small steam engine was attached to an iron bicycle frame in this French design from the 1860s.

*Safer than early high-wheelers, this bicycle was powered by a rear-wheel chain that allowed the **rider to sit closer to the ground.***

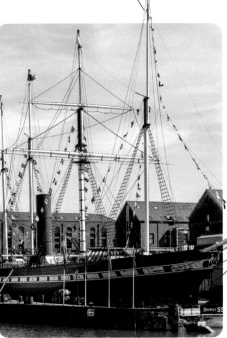

Steam motor bicycle

Swift safety bicycle

SS *Great Britain*

This engine ran on the Indian rail line known as the "Toy Train," which took passengers 48 miles (78 km) through the mountains.

*Set up in 1877, the Natal Government Railways **connected eastern areas of present-day South Africa.***

Darjeeling Himalayan Railway

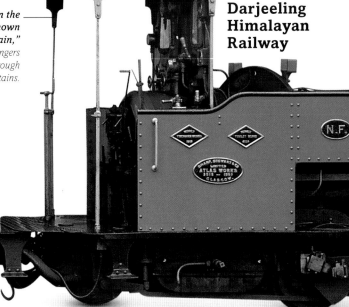

Natal Government Railways

From the 1750s, new forms of transportation by road, rail, air, and sea opened up the world as never before. This age of invention saw groundbreaking designs transformed into a reality. By the 20th century, bicycles, cars, boats, trains, and planes offered more and more people opportunities for travel.

Early versions of popular modes of transportation were sometimes dangerous. On the road, the **Penny Farthing** bicycle of the 1870s featured a precariously high seat, risky for both rider and pedestrians. The **Swift safety bicycle** and other similar, safer designs soon replaced it. In 1885, German engineer Karl Benz

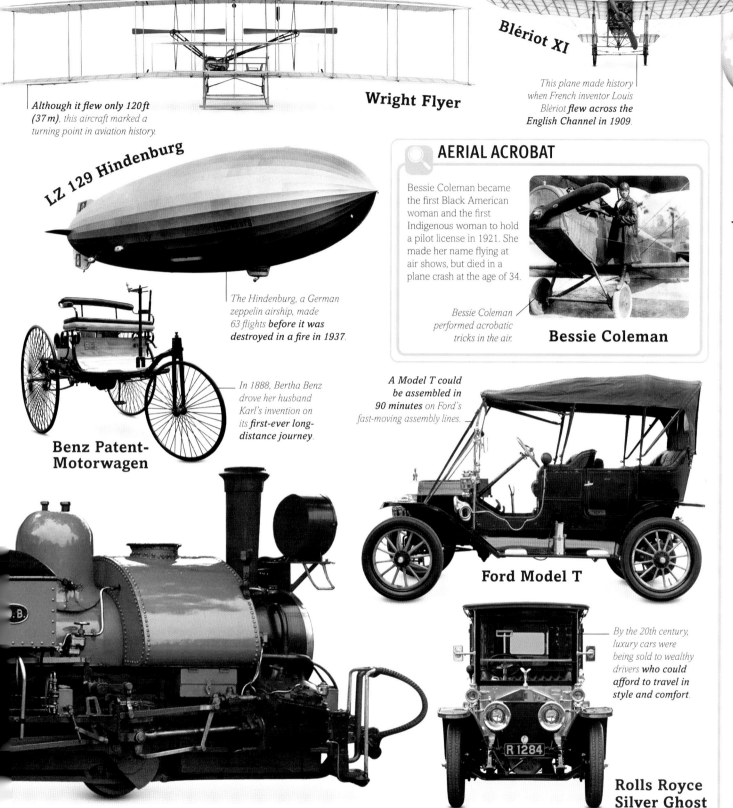

Wright Flyer

Although it flew only 120 ft (37 m), this aircraft marked a turning point in aviation history.

Blériot XI

This plane made history when French inventor Louis Blériot flew across the English Channel in 1909.

LZ 129 Hindenburg

The Hindenburg, a German zeppelin airship, made 63 flights before it was destroyed in a fire in 1937.

AERIAL ACROBAT

Bessie Coleman became the first Black American woman and the first Indigenous woman to hold a pilot license in 1921. She made her name flying at air shows, but died in a plane crash at the age of 34.

Bessie Coleman performed acrobatic tricks in the air.

Bessie Coleman

Benz Patent-Motorwagen

In 1888, Bertha Benz drove her husband Karl's invention on its first-ever long-distance journey.

A Model T could be assembled in 90 minutes on Ford's fast-moving assembly lines.

Ford Model T

By the 20th century, luxury cars were being sold to wealthy drivers who could afford to travel in style and comfort.

Rolls Royce Silver Ghost

built the **Benz Patent-Motorwagen**, the first gasoline-powered car. American businessman Henry Ford went on to develop mass-produced cars, selling 15 million of his **Ford Model T** by 1927. In 1903, American brothers Orville and Wilbur Wright turned their eyes to the skies, mastering powered flight in their **Wright Flyer**.

In India, meanwhile, the **Darjeeling Himalayan Railway** connected a remote region to the rest of the country, while at sea, the ***SS Great Britain***, the first propeller-powered steamship to cross the Atlantic, ushered in an age of faster, cheaper international travel in 1843.

THE MODERN WORLD

The Modern World

Two horrific world wars dominated the first half of the 20th century. New conflicts and fears arose in the late 20th century, but technology also advanced in leaps and bounds, and new ideas of freedom and equality emerged.

The first half of the 20th century was dominated by two of the bloodiest conflicts in history. Weakened by their involvement in these wars, the European powers gradually lost control of their overseas empires in the second half of the century. They could no longer stop anti-colonial independence movements, leading to the emergence of many new independent nations around the world. By the early 1980s, most colonies had won their independence.

Global warfare

The two world wars were unlike any wars that had gone before. Each of them spread to almost every continent, as the colonial powers fought each other, often in their overseas territories. New vehicles changed the nature of the battlefield, with fighter planes taking to the air and heavily armored tanks rolling over trenches. The invention and use of atomic bombs at the end of World War II changed the face of warfare forever.

WORLD WAR II US STAGHOUND ARMORED CAR
World War II saw many technological advances, particularly in transportation. This armored car was built by the US, but only saw active service with British and British colonial forces.

The death toll of these wars was immense. Taking both wars together, at least 70 million people were killed—around 6 million of these were Jews who died in the genocide known as the Holocaust during World War II.

The Cold War

The US and the Soviet Union became the new global superpowers after World War II, but soon became fierce rivals due to their opposing political and economic systems. Instead of declaring war against each other, the two nations fought a "Cold War," in which they each backed different sides in various conflicts around the world, and threatened each other with growing stockpiles of nuclear weapons. The two nations also competed with technology, each trying to get the upper hand in the "Space Race." The Soviets put the first satellite in space, as well as

WORLD WAR I CEMETERY
Around 8.5 million soldiers lost their lives during World War I, two-thirds of them in battle. Another 21 million soldiers were wounded.

the first human being, but the US was the first nation to land a person on the moon. The Cold War finally ended in 1991 with the collapse of the Soviet Union.

New freedoms

In the 1960s, the Cold War played out against a background of antiwar protests and campaigns to ban nuclear weapons. These were often spearheaded by young people, who for the first time were able to see the horrors of war on their televisions at home, and who rejected its violence. Many young people wanted to live in a different way from their parents, and rebelled against the older generation.

At the same time, members of the US civil rights movement fought against the unfair laws that allowed racial discrimination against Black Americans. The feminist movement, which fought for equal rights for women, also saw a surge of activism during the 1960s.

HIPPIE VAN

In the 1960s, Volkswagen Buses became popular vehicles among hippies, who decorated them with symbols of peace. Hippies were young people who wanted to experiment with new ways of living. They cared about the environment, and believed in nonviolence.

The Information Age

New technologies developed at the end of the 20th century and in the 21st century have given us new freedoms. With the emergence of the internet, we can find information at the touch of a button. The development of the microchip allows us to carry phones and computers with us wherever we go. These new technologies have become essential to our daily lives, making them easier and safer. However, since the 1970s, scientists have become increasingly aware that Earth's climate is warming due to emissions from cars, farming, and industry. Governments have agreed to limit global warming to a rise of just 2.7°F (1.5°C), but it is not clear how they are going to do this.

MODERN DUBAI

The city of Dubai in the United Arab Emirates, with its skyline of ultra-modern skyscrapers, has made itself a center for technological innovation and research.

World War I

German airships or zeppelins dropped bombs on British towns and cities.

Zeppelin

Serbian student Gavrilo Princip shot Archduke Franz Ferdinand of Austria-Hungary with this pistol.

Assassin's weapon

Issued to British soldiers, **this rifle could fire up to 15 rounds a minute.**

Lee Enfield Mark l rifle

Prussian Unteroffizier uniform

Used by German soldiers during trench battles, **these stick grenades had a 5–7 second delay before explosion.**

This deadly battlefield weapon **could fire 400 bullets per minute, with a range of up to 5,900 ft (1,800 m).**

MG08 Maxim machine gun

Stick grenade

Portable telephones **allowed soldiers to receive orders quickly on the battlefield.**

Deployed in 1918, the British Mark V could travel over trenches and was resistant to gunfire.

Mark V tank

Soldiers who served in the **Prussian infantry of the German army wore this green uniform.**

Field telephone set

World War I was a global conflict from 1914 to 1918, fought between two alliances of countries—the Central Powers and the Allies. The war spread to almost every continent and was one of the bloodiest conflicts in history, leading to the deaths of more than 20 million people.

The Central Powers, which included Germany and Austria-Hungary, and the Allies, which included the UK, France, Japan, and the US, were bitter rivals. The assassination of an archduke from Austria-Hungary in June 1914 triggered an international conflict. Both sides employed lethal modern weapons, such as the **Lee Enfield rifle**, the **stick**

Soldiers from colonized regions were transported to fight for European countries, such as these Indian soldiers fighting for Britain in the Middle East.

Troops from colonies

Eugene Bullard, the first Black combat pilot, flew for the French air force after the US Army rejected him because of his race.

Eugene Bullard

Fought from February 21 to December 15, 1916, **the longest battle of the war** saw the deaths of more than 300,000 soldiers.

Battle of Verdun

British Sopwith Triplane

World War I was one of the first wars to use aircraft in large numbers, which included fighter planes battling at heights of up to 12,000 ft (3,660 m).

Treaty of Versailles

This treaty placed the responsibility of the war on Germany and forced it to pay war damages to the Allies.

grenade, and the **Maxim machine gun**. In Europe, both sides dug trenches that became their bases for long-drawn-out conflicts, such as the **Battle of Verdun**. However, the invention of tanks that could cross trenches, such as the **Mark V**, changed how the war was fought. Fighting spread to Asia, Africa, and the Middle East, and European powers shipped **troops from colonies** to fight in these locations. In the Pacific, the Japanese Navy captured German colonies, weakening the Central Powers. In 1918, the Central Powers were defeated and forced to sign treaties, such as the **Treaty of Versailles**, to end the war.

The rise of communism

An uncaring ruler, Romanov ruler Czar Nicholas II lived in luxury with his family while the people suffered.

Romanov family

The Russian Revolution

*The red star—a symbol of communism in Russia—became the emblem of the **Russian army, called the Red Army**.*

Red Army cap

The revolution spread across Russia after starving, peaceful protesters were killed by Czar Nicholas II's guards on January 22, 1905, now known as Bloody Sunday.

The Cultural Revolution was started by Mao Zedong in 1966 to revive communist values—leading to attacks on his opponents and anyone thought to be anticommunist.

*This Soviet sculpture idealizes **the worker with the hammer and** the kolkhoz (farmer) with the sickle.*

Worker and Kolkhoz Woman

Vladimir Lenin (right) was the first communist leader of Russia and helped create the Soviet Union, but after Lenin's death, Joseph Stalin (left) grabbed power and became a dictator.

Russian revolutionaries

In the early 20th century, a new political system—communism—began gathering momentum. It promised a society with no class divisions and where everything was owned by the people, not individuals. This idea appealed to many, sparking revolutions across Europe, Asia, and the Caribbean.

Rising up as poverty raged in the country, **Russian revolutionaries** deposed the **Romanov family** in 1917, and set up a communist government. Communism spread to Russia's neighbors as well, and in 1922, together they created the Union of Soviet Socialist Republics (USSR), or the Soviet Union. The ideals of communism also reached

The revolution ended dynastic rule in China, and empowered the common people—which later led to the rise of communism in China.

Xinhai Revolution

The Chinese Civil War (1945–1949) was fought between the Nationalists, led by Chiang Kai-shek, and the Communist Party, led by Mao Zedong.

Chinese Civil War

Pocket-size, the Little Red Book contains 267 quotes from Mao Zedong's speeches and was required reading for everyone during the Cultural Revolution.

Little Red Book

革命师生是同一战壕的战方

The slogan on this poster from 1974 says "Revolutionary teachers and students are comrades in arms in the same trenches."

Chinese communist poster

Strongly supported by the Soviet Union, Polish communist leader Bierut was the president of Poland from 1947 to 1952.

Boleslaw Bierut

The Cultural Revolution

Ho Chi Minh fought to unite North and South Vietnam under communist rule but died before Vietnam's unification in 1976.

Ho Chi Minh

For two years, Castro fought a guerrilla war in the Sierra Maestra mountains against Cuba's corrupt president, Fulgencio Batista.

Fidel Castro

Che Guevara

Argentinian revolutionary and medical student Ernesto "Che" Guevara helped Fidel Castro defeat the dictatorship in Cuba.

China, and after Mao Zedong's victory in the **Chinese Civil War**, China became a one-party communist state in 1949. **Ho Chi Minh** of North Vietnam also believed in communism, and in reunification with South Vietnam, which led to the Vietnam War from 1955. In the Caribbean, **Fidel Castro** liberated Cuba from an oppressive regime in 1959 to set up a communist government. Parts of Europe became communist under Soviet influence after World War II. But the collapse of the Soviet Union in 1991 ended communism in Eastern Europe. However, other nations, such as Cuba, Laos, and North Korea, are still communist.

Women's voting rights

*British suffragette Emily Davison fought passionately for women's suffrage, and was **arrested several times** for throwing stones and starting fires.*

Emily Davison

*In 1893, all women in New Zealand, including Indigenous women, **were given the right to vote**.*

Women voting in New Zealand

Emmeline Pankhurst

*Leading British suffragette Emmeline Pankhurst **was often arrested during protests**.*

*Susan B. Anthony was a **leading activist** in the women's suffrage movement in the US.*

Susan B. Anthony

*Elizabeth C. Stanton was a prominent **campaigner** for women's rights in the US.*

*Sojourner Truth fought for Black women to be **recognized** in the US suffrage movement.*

Sojourner Truth

Elizabeth C. Stanton

In the 18th and 19th centuries, new nations were formed on principles of democracy, but women did not have the vote. Widespread sexism led men in power to believe women did not have the intelligence or emotional skills to vote. But many women disagreed, and fought hard for the right to vote.

In the UK, female activists for voting rights (known as "suffrage") campaigned from the 1860s onward. Those who were willing to break the law, such as Sophia Duleep Singh, **Emmeline Pankhurst**, and **Emily Davison** became known as "suffragettes." Some of them were sent to Holloway Prison for protesting.

A prominent feminist activist, Funmilayo Ransome-Kuti fought for women's rights in Nigeria.

Funmilayo Ransome-Kuti

Holloway brooch

Designed by Sylvia Pankhurst, the brooch was given to British suffragettes who were sent to Holloway Prison for their protests.

The leading women's rights group in China was set up in 1949 following the Communist revolution.

All China Women's Federation

Japanese feminist Shidzue Katō was one of the first women elected to the Japanese Parliament.

Woman Suffrage Party pennant

Votes For Women

The Woman Suffrage Party was founded in 1909 in New York, and had 100,000 members by 1915.

Women's rights organizations gave medals to British suffragettes who spent time in prison—many of who went on hunger strike while in jail.

Suffragette medal

Shidzue Katō

South Africa Women's anti-pass campaign

In 1956, around 20,000 women protested against laws that forced Black women to carry passes that stopped them from moving freely around the country.

Chilean lawyer Elena Caffarena devoted her life to achieving women's suffrage, which was granted in Chile in 1949.

Elena Caffarena

In the US, activists such as **Elizabeth C. Stanton**, Carrie Chapman Catt, and **Susan B. Anthony** campaigned for the vote and faced arrest for their actions. White campaigners often failed to stand up for the rights of Black women, but Black activists, such as **Sojourner Truth**, fought for voting rights and property rights.

The first nation to grant all women the vote in national elections was **New Zealand**, in 1893. **Shidzue Katō** led the fight for women's rights in the 1920s and 1930s in Japan, while **Funmilayo Ransome-Kuti** fought for the vote in colonial Nigeria in the 1940s and 1950s.

America between the wars

Flapper fashion

The Charleston allowed people to dance energetically with its lively mix of solo and paired moves.

Charleston dance

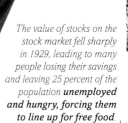

The Jazz Age

A trumpeter and singer, Louis Armstrong **became a celebrity** *as the popularity of jazz music soared in the 1920s.*

After decades of wearing tight corsets, women loved the **loose** fit and shorter length of flapper clothing.

The value of stocks on the stock market fell sharply in 1929, leading to many people losing their savings and leaving 25 percent of the population **unemployed** and hungry, forcing them to line up for free food.

Mobs of white residents burned down Black-owned businesses and homes in the Black neighborhood of Greenwood in Tulsa in 1921, killing around 300 Black people.

Chrysler Building

Tulsa Race Massacre

Built in the Art Deco style popular in the 1920s and 1930s, **the Chrysler Building** in New York City is one of the US's early skyscrapers.

The Great Depression

The period between the two world wars was a time of extreme highs and lows for the US. Exciting new music and fashion made people optimistic about the future, but this optimism was shattered by natural and economic disasters and racial violence.

There was a sense of freedom in the US after World War I (1914–1918) ended. The **Jazz Age** granted musicians a chance to experiment, with many Black players blending African rhythms with European harmonies. Comfortable **flapper fashion** meant women could move around more easily, and dances, such as the **Charleston**, were carefree and joyful. Some people, however,

US mass migration

*A drought in the 1930s left the Great Plains dusty and barren, **forcing thousands of agricultural workers to migrate west** to California in search of work.*

Baseball legend Babe Ruth's teams won the World Series seven times from 1915 to 1932.

Babe Ruth

Babe Ruth was known by baseball fans as "**The Sultan of Swat**."

Zora Neale Hurston

Black author Zora Neale Hurston wrote about the stories of Black people in the United States, the Caribbean, and Central America.

*As radios became affordable, listeners had **easy access to news and entertainment at home**.*

Radio

*Alcohol barrels were confiscated and drained into **sewers** during government raids, so many Americans learned how to make alcohol secretly at home.*

Prohibition

*Built during the Great Depression, the Hoover Dam project **provided jobs for thousands of unemployed people**.*

Hoover Dam

Roosevelt's plan was called the "New Deal" and increased employment, helped the economy recover, and also reformed the banking sector.

Franklin D. Roosevelt

thought that there was too much freedom. They supported the government's ban on drinking and selling alcohol—known as **prohibition**—even though it failed to stop alcohol manufacture and illegal "speakeasy" bars. Black people continued to be discriminated against and suffered horrific hate crimes, such as the **Tulsa Race Massacre**. The 1920s delivered another low when a huge stock market crash in 1929 triggered the **Great Depression**. Millions lost their jobs overnight and were forced into poverty. When **Franklin D. Roosevelt** became president in 1933, he implemented a financial plan that created jobs and reversed the country's hardships—but only just before World War II broke out in Europe in 1939.

World War II

Invasion of France

German troops marched victoriously through the streets of Paris after taking over France.

Women in factories

Many women joined the war effort by working in factories, such as this mechanic helping to build a B-25 Bomber.

More than 150,000 Allied soldiers landed on the beaches of Normandy, France, on June 6, 1944.

German ration card

Ration cards gave citizens access to vital supplies, such as food and clothing.

Many nations involved in the war awarded medals to recognize courage in battle, including the Silver Star—a US Armed Forces medal.

US Silver Star medal

Young children wore colorful "Mickey Mouse" gas masks, made from a thin material.

Some soldiers on the battlefront received treats from home.

Gas mask

Ration can

Attack on Pearl Harbor

After the devastation of World War I, there was little appetite for fresh conflict. But when Nazi Germany invaded Poland in 1939, the Allies—Britain, France, and later the Soviet Union and the US—fought back. World War II became one of the deadliest conflicts in history, causing about 50 million deaths.

Early in the war, Germany seized territories across Europe, and by 1940, it had **invaded France**. As the war spread, civilians were greatly affected. With more men joining the war, more **women worked in factories** and on farms. Supplies of food and clothing became limited, and people carried **gas masks** for fear of

D-Day landings

Named after the city where they trained, the Tuskegee airmen were the US military's first Black flying squadron.

Tuskegee airmen

Japan's Pearl Harbor ambush killed more than 2,400 people and drew the US into the war.

Japanese soldiers kept prayer cards in their pockets to comfort them through the horrors of war.

Japanese prayer card

*This picture of **Soviet soldiers atop Germany's** Reichstag (parliament) building became a symbol of Nazi defeat.*

Fall of Berlin

poisonous gas attacks from enemy planes. In 1941, Japan (an ally of Germany) launched a surprise **attack on Pearl Harbor**, a US Naval base. The US now entered the war, fighting intense air battles with Japan over the Pacific Islands. In 1944, the Allies began their **D-Day landings**, to liberate western Europe from German control. By May 1945, Soviet troops had entered Germany from the east and brought about the **fall of Berlin**, ending Nazi Germany. But it was only when Japan surrendered—after the US detonated atomic bombs on its cities— that this deadly conflict was finally over.

The Holocaust

The Nazi Party

The Nazi Party blamed Jews for Germany's economic problems, and spread lies to make ordinary citizens hate this community.

The passports of Jewish people were stamped with a "J," making it difficult for them to hide their identity or leave Nazi-occupied territories.

Jewish passports

Rioters looted Jewish businesses, destroyed synagogues, and killed around 100 Jewish people over two nights in November 1938.

November Pogrom

Kindertransport means **"children's transport"** in German.

About 10,000 children from Europe escaped Nazi persecution by traveling to the UK before the start of World War II.

Kindertransport

The cramped Warsaw Ghetto was divided into two parts, which were linked by a foot bridge to prevent Jews from using the main streets of the city.

Warsaw Ghetto

This badge with the word "Jew" in Dutch was worn by Jews living in Nazi-occupied Netherlands.

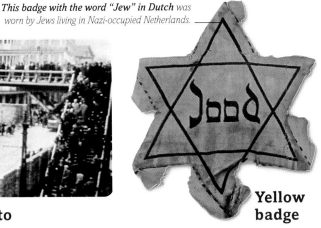

Yellow badge

During World War II, Germany's Nazi Party and its collaborators killed an estimated six million Jewish people—a genocide that came to be known as the Holocaust. Jews from across Europe were either shot or sent to camps, where many died from starvation or disease, or in gas chambers.

When the **Nazi Party** came to power in 1933, there was a rise in discrimination against Jews, whose rights and citizenship were gradually stripped away. Jewish homes and businesses were targeted during the **November Pogrom** (also called Kristallnacht). Fearing for their children, European Jews appealed to other countries for help—in the UK, many Jewish

Ghetto money

The Theresienstadt Ghetto of the Czech Republic had a currency that could be used to buy items but had no value outside the ghetto.

Zyklon B was a pesticide for killing insects, but the Nazis used it to poison millions of people in gas chambers.

Gas chamber chemical

In April 1945, the US Army freed more than 32,000 prisoners from the Dachau concentration camp.

Liberation of camps

Auschwitz

Jews arriving at Auschwitz were separated from their families, and either killed or selected for hard labor.

Between 1945 and 1946, many Nazi Party officials were caught and tried for their role in World War II and the Holocaust.

Post-war justice

This Holocaust memorial in Germany is made up of thousands of concrete blocks, its similarity to a graveyard bringing to mind a sense of the lives lost.

Holocaust memorial

ANNE FRANK

Anne Frank was a German-Jewish teenager who went into hiding with her family for two years, before they were found by the Nazis. She eventually died in a concentration camp. Her father survived and was able to publish her diary, which gave an insight into the life of a young girl living under Nazi oppression.

children were rescued in the **Kindertransport** effort. As Nazi Germany won battles in World War II, Jews in Nazi-occupied territories were forced to live in overcrowded ghettos. From here, they were sent to concentration camps, such as **Auschwitz**, where they faced enslaved labor, starvation, and diseases caused by terrible living conditions, leading to many deaths. The Nazis also sent the Roma and Sinti people, prisoners of war, homosexual people, and disabled people to the camps. As the war progressed, the Nazis began killing the camp prisoners in large numbers, using **gas chambers** or shooting them. By the time Allied forces freed those who were left, millions had already died.

Modern warfare

This explosive device was designed to target enemy soldiers during an ambush attack.

Claymore mine

Apache helicopter

The AH-64 Apache two-seater attack helicopter *is used in aerial combat around the world.*

F-16 fighter jet

*Known as the "Fighting Falcon," this single-seat, single-engine fighter **participates in aerial combat and ground strikes**.*

MQ-9 Reaper

This armed aircraft flies without a pilot and is controlled remotely to hit enemy targets or collect information during conflict.

Ghillie suit

*A camouflaged outfit designed to merge with dense foliage **makes it hard to spot an armed soldier**.*

Barrett M82 sniper rifle

*Developed in the USSR in the 1940s, the AK-47 assault rifle **remains the most widely used rifle worldwide**.*

*Used extensively in the **Vietnam War**, the M60 needs a team of three soldiers to carry, load, and fire it.*

*This long-range sniper rifle can **fire straight through concrete and brick walls**.*

AK-47 rifle

M60 machine gun

Weaponry has developed on an unprecedented scale since World War II. The introduction of new equipment, transportation, firearms, and artillery in the 21st century, coupled with computerized missiles and remote launches, have resulted in the most advanced weaponry ever seen.

Advanced versions of handheld weapons are still used by armed forces today. The **AK-47 rifle** remains a battlefield staple, the **M60 machine gun** blasts 500 rounds a minute, and the **Barrett M82 sniper rifle** is used by at least 50 countries. Even more devastating is the shoulder-launched **Javelin antitank missile**

Supersonic missile

The Indian Army's BrahMos cruise missile can be **launched from a truck, submarine, ship, or aircraft**.

This Soviet artillery gun is loaded by **hand** and fires with devastating effect.

152 mm Gun-Howitzer M1955

The M1955 can hit targets as far as **15 miles (24 km)**.

Type 96B tank

This robust Chinese tank can set vehicles alight with one shot and withstand attacks from heavy weaponry.

Despite its great size, this US antitank missile is lightweight and **can be launched from a soldier's shoulder**.

This jet-powered, **long-range cruise missile** is typically launched from ships and submarines.

Tomahawk missile

Javelin antitank missile

deployed to target tanks since 1996. Ambush tactics allow soldiers to attack the enemy without warning. **Ghillie suits** provide the latest camouflage, while hidden **Claymore mines** explode across enemy lines. Although ground soldiers are still involved in conflict, military attacks are now usually launched from aircraft such as **F-16 fighter jets** and **Apache helicopters**. Satellite technology allows conflicts to take place remotely over long distances, with the **MQ-9 Reaper** flown by remote control and **Tomahawk missiles** fired from ships and submarines miles away.

Decolonization

Pan-African flag

Designed by Jamaican activist Marcus Garvey, **this flag became a symbol of Black unity during the era of decolonization.**

Una Marson was a Jamaican activist who fought for decolonization in Africa and the Caribbean, and civil rights for Black people in Britain.

Activist and politician Aimé Césaire proposed that Martinique should change from a French colony to an integral part of France.

Una Marson was **the first Black radio producer** for the BBC.

Ghana's independence struggle, led by Kwame Nkrumah (center), **inspired many other African nations to fight for their independence.**

Una Marson

Aimé Césaire

Ghanaian independence

Indian flag

Pakistani flag

Mahatma Gandhi was determined to free India from British rule but refused to use violence to do so.

Mahatma Gandhi

The British divided **newly independent India into two states—India and Pakistan.**

By the mid-20th century, European empires had been weakened by World War II. They could no longer contain or stop the growing anti-colonial and independence movements in Africa and Asia. After years of struggle, most of these colonies were able to gain their independence before the end of the century.

India was one of the first European colonies to become independent, in 1947. This followed a long period of anti-colonial resistance by figures such as **Mahatma Gandhi**. Ten years later, **Ghana** became the first Black African country to gain independence from a European empire, winning its freedom from the British in

A scholar and activist, *Eric Williams* became the first prime minister of independent Trinidad and Tobago.

Eric Williams

Jomo Kenyatta

Independent Kenya's first president, *Jomo Kenyatta* was imprisoned for eight years during the Kenyan struggle for freedom.

THE FIRST PRESIDENT OF KENYA · MZEE JOMO KENYATTA

10 CENTS MALAYA KELANTAN

The British colony of Malaya in Southeast Asia became part of a federation of independent states in 1957, before becoming **the state of Malaysia in 1963**.

Independent Malaya stamp

Bibi Titi Mohammed was an influential anti-colonial activist who fought against British rule in Tanzania.

Bibi Titi Mohammed

🔍 **DECOLONIZATION WARS**

Struggles for independence sometimes involved violence. Algeria fought a seven-year-long guerrilla war against France to gain independence. Portugal fought for 13 years to keep its colonies in Angola, Guinea-Bissau, and Mozambique, while the 15-year Rhodesian Bush War saw Zimbabwe's Black majority fight against rule by a white minority.

Samora Machel fought in the Portuguese Colonial War before becoming the first president of independent Mozambique in 1975.

Samora Machel

1957. In East Africa, **Jomo Kenyatta** led the struggle for Kenyan independence from Britain, which was achieved in 1963. Other nations followed and by 1981 most former colonies in Africa and Asia had become independent. In the Caribbean, there was disagreement over what decolonization should look like. For example, **Eric Williams** of Trinidad and Tobago advocated full independence from Britain, while in Martinique, **Aimé Césaire** instead argued that Martinicans should become fully fledged citizens of France.

THE PARTITION OF INDIA
In 1947, British colonial rule over India came to an end. At the stroke of midnight on August 15, the country was divided into two nations based on religion—Hindu-majority India and Muslim-majority Pakistan. This sudden event, known as the Partition, led to chaos at train stations as millions of people attempted to flee across newly made borders amid widespread violence.

The announcement for the Partition happened so quickly that many Muslims in India and Hindus and Sikhs in Pakistan found themselves unwelcome in their own land. Nearly 15 million people were displaced from their homes and became refugees. Large-scale violence and riots also erupted between religious groups, and many people were killed.

The refugee crisis lasted for the next few years, and the violent history of Partition continues to affect the relationship between India and Pakistan to this day. In 1971, Pakistan was further divided into two separate countries, present-day Pakistan and Bangladesh.

The Cold War

The Yalta Conference

British prime minister Winston Churchill, US president Franklin D. Roosevelt, and Soviet leader Joseph Stalin met in 1945 at Yalta, Crimea, to plan Germany's future.

*In 1948, Soviet forces surrounded West Berlin, forcing the US and its allies to **air drop food and supplies to the residents for 11 months**.*

The Berlin Airlift

Communist North Korea invaded US ally South Korea in 1950, which prompted the US to come to South Korea's defense, resulting in a war that lasted three years.

The Korean War

*The decade-long war between communist North Vietnam and US-supported South Vietnam **killed up to three million Vietnamese people, and around 58,000 US soldiers**.*

The Vietnam War

*US president John F. Kennedy reacted to the Soviet Union's placement of nuclear weapons in Cuba **by ordering nuclear weapons to be readied for war**.*

The Cuban Missile Crisis

Duck and cover drills were held regularly in US schools to teach students what to do in case of a nuclear attack.

Duck and cover

The US and the Soviet Union emerged as global superpowers after World War II ended in 1945, and soon became rivals. Instead of declaring war and fighting directly, they fought a "cold war" from 1946 to 1991, through alliances with other nations and the threat of nuclear weapons.

The US and the Soviet Union were run on opposing political and economic systems. The US embraced capitalism, in which businesses are run for profit, while the Soviet Union adopted communism, under which all property is owned by the state. The friction between these two worldviews played out through conflicts in many countries, including **Korea**,

Apollo patch

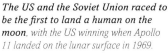

The US and the Soviet Union raced to be the first to land a human on the moon, with the US winning when Apollo 11 landed on the lunar surface in 1969.

Angola's independence from Portugal in 1975 was followed by a bloody civil war that lasted for more than 20 years, in which rival factions were backed by the US and the Soviet Union.

The Angolan Civil War

*Both sides spied on each other to gain information using new technology, such as this **Soviet spy ring with a hidden camera**.*

Spy camera

American 10-year-old Samantha Smith was invited to Moscow in response to a letter she wrote to the leader of the Soviet Union in 1982, becoming known as "America's youngest ambassador."

Samantha Smith

*In 1979, Soviet soldiers were sent to **Afghanistan** to back the communist Afghan government, which was fighting anticommunist Muslim forces backed by the US.*

The Soviet–Afghan War

*Soviet leader Mikhail Gorbachev and US president Ronald Reagan signed a treaty in 1987 to **eliminate their stock of missiles that could carry nuclear warheads**.*

Washington Summit

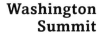

*The Berlin Wall, which since 1961 had divided Soviet-controlled East Berlin from West Berlin, fell in 1989, signaling **the beginning of the end of the Cold War**.*

Fall of the Berlin Wall

Vietnam, **Angola**, and **Afghanistan**. The **Cuban Missile Crisis** of 1962 nearly led to direct conflict between the two powers, when the Soviet Union placed nuclear missiles in Cuba, only 90 miles (144 km) from the US mainland. The world was gripped with the fear of a nuclear war, and people in the US were taught methods such as **duck and cover** to protect them in case of an attack. Steps toward peace were slow. In 1987, leaders of the two nations met at the **Washington Summit** and agreed to reduce their store of weapons. But it was only after the Soviet Union collapsed in 1991 that the Cold War finally ended.

Codes and espionage

Smoke signals, a form of communication for some Indigenous peoples of the Americas, were **created by holding a blanket over a fire.**

Smoke signal

This device helps to easily encode a message into the Caesar cipher by rotating the outer and inner disks.

Caesar cipher device

J.H.S. WARD
LONDON

James Armistead Lafayette was an enslaved Black man who spied on the **British** during the American Revolution.

James Armistead Lafayette

A telegraph transmitter is a 19th-century device **used to send messages using Morse Code.**

The Germans used the Enigma **to relay military orders** and coordinate attacks.

Telegraph transmitter

The cipher reel was **used by the armies of the** pro-slavery Confederate States to relay messages during the American Civil War.

Section II.—THE CYPHER.

British mathematician **Alan Turing** developed a machine that could break the Enigma machine code.

American Civil War cipher reel

Alan Turing

Klappe schliessen   ENIGMA

Enigma machine

People have often used codes to send and receive important messages. Rulers and armies have also used espionage, or spying, to get access to information about the secrets, strengths, and weaknesses of their enemies. Over the years, forms of code and espionage have evolved across cultures.

Codes have been in use since ancient times. The **Caesar cipher**, named after the Roman leader Julius Caesar, works by substituting each letter in the original message with letters located further down the alphabet. Many cultures, including the Diné and Apache peoples of North America, used **smoke signals** to send important

Food tin

During World War I, spies used food cans to hide important documents such as maps.

Noor Inayat Khan was a World War II British officer of Indian descent who operated as a spy in German-occupied France.

Yoshiko Kawashima was a Chinese princess who became a spy for Japan during the Second Sino-Japanese War.

Josephine Baker was a Black American entertainer during World War II who spied on the Germans in occupied France.

Noor Inayat Khan

Yoshiko Kawashima

Secret compartments in shoe heels allow spies to carry concealed items.

Concealed radio

Spies sometimes hide radios in household items to help them send messages without detection.

Hollow coins are used to transport small objects such as microfilms and flash drives.

Heel with concealed compartment

Josephine Baker

INTELLIGENCE AGENCIES

Today, many countries have dedicated organizations focused on espionage. These include the US's Central Intelligence Agency (CIA), the UK's MI5 and MI6, and Russia's Federal Security Service (FSB), which was formerly the KGB.

CIA seal　　**KGB seal**

Hollow coins

Spy cameras can be hidden in items as ordinary as a lighter.

The lipstick guns used by Russian KGB operatives could fire only a single bullet.

Lighter spy camera

Lipstick gun

messages, such as warnings, over long distances. Codes and spycraft evolved greatly in the 20th century. During World War II, Germany developed the **Enigma machine**, which could create a very complex code. It took the Allies a long time and many code breakers, led by **Alan Turing**, to break it. Spies, such as **Noor Inayat Khan**, went into enemy territory, from where they sent back information using codes and special devices, such as **hollow coins** and **concealed radios**. To protect themselves, spies also often carried weapons disguised as everyday items, such as **lipstick guns**.

The US civil rights movement

Groups of Black and white activists rode buses together through the US South to challenge segregation on public transportation.

FREEDOM RIDE
CORE
Freedom Riders

Laws enforcing racial segregation meant it was illegal for Black and white Americans to share the same public spaces.

In many states in the US, it was illegal for Black and white children to go to the same schools.

School segregation

Martin Luther King, Jr., a prominent Black activist, led a march of 250,000 people in Washington, D.C., in 1963, calling for racial equality.

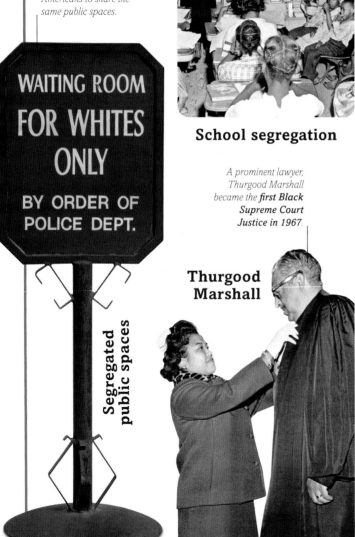

WAITING ROOM
FOR WHITES ONLY
BY ORDER OF POLICE DEPT.

Segregated public spaces

*A prominent lawyer, Thurgood Marshall became the **first Black Supreme Court Justice in 1967.***

Thurgood Marshall

Martin Luther King, Jr.

In 1619, the first recorded group of enslaved Africans arrived in North America. Slavery was abolished in the US in 1865, but Black Americans continued to face huge amounts of discrimination in their everyday lives. They fought back, culminating in a major civil rights movement in the 20th century.

By the 1950s, much of the US remained segregated, meaning that Black and white people were often not allowed to use the same services and **public spaces**. This segregation was upheld by a set of policies and laws known as Jim Crow laws. However, many people challenged these laws. Some, such as **Martin Luther**

In 1955, Rosa Parks refused to give up her bus seat to a white passenger—the following year segregation on buses was ended.

Rosa Parks

The Black Panther Party was a revolutionary activist group that was formed to protect Black people from police violence.

POWER TO THE PEOPLE

Black Panther Party badge

Malcolm X believed that Black people must fight for their rights, including the right to vote, by any means necessary.

Malcolm X

In 1960, Ruby Bridges was one of the first Black children to go to what had once been a white-only school, helping to bring an end to segregation.

Desegregation

🔍 BLACK LIVES MATTER

The Black Lives Matter (BLM) movement is a 21st-century activist movement that campaigns for Black people around the world to have full access to their human rights. In particular, they argue that Black people should not be treated unfairly by the police. It is a decentralized movement, meaning that there is no official leader.

In 2020, there were Black Lives Matter protests around the world following the death of George Floyd, who was killed by a police officer in the United States.

A BLM protest

King, Jr., and **Malcolm X**, fought by campaigning and delivering speeches. Others, such as Claudette Colvin, **Rosa Parks**, and the **Freedom Riders**, publicly refused to obey unjust laws in acts of civil disobedience. Yet others fought the laws in court with cases such as *Brown v. Board of Education*, which led to a decision by the US Supreme Court that found **school segregation** unlawful. As a result of all this activism, many discriminatory laws and policies were overturned. Even so, racial discrimination still exists in the US today. Many activists, including those in the **Black Lives Matter** movement, continue to fight against it.

Computers

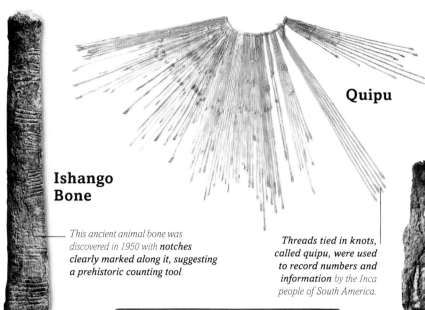

Quipu

*This water-powered clock, designed by Islamic scholar Ismail al-Jazari, is **an automated machine that tells the time by following a series of steps**.*

Ishango Bone

*This ancient animal bone was discovered in 1950 with **notches clearly marked along it**, suggesting a prehistoric counting tool.*

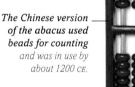

*Threads tied in knots, called quipu, were used to **record numbers and information** by the Inca people of South America.*

*The Antikythera Mechanism was an ancient Greek machine that might have been used to **predict star positions and solar eclipses**.*

Antikythera Mechanism

*Completed in 1945, ENIAC (Electronic Numerical Integrator and Computer) **was a groundbreaking computer that weighed a staggering 33 tons**.*

The Chinese version of the abacus used beads for counting and was in use by about 1200 CE.

ENIAC

Suanpan

COMPUTING PIONEERS

The trailblazers who revolutionized the field of computer programming were often women. British mathematician Ada Lovelace became the first computer programmer in the 19th century by writing sets of rules for computers to carry out problem-solving tasks. In the 1960s, Black American scientist Katherine Johnson worked out calculations to send NASA spacecraft on correct trajectories during spaceflight.

Ada Lovelace   Katherine Johnson

As far back as prehistoric times, the first counting devices were in use for basic mathematics. However, it wasn't until the 20th century that computers became the complex machines that we know today—with the invention of the microchip transforming what computers can do.

The **Ishango Bone**, found in the Democratic Republic of the Congo, is one of the earliest examples of tools used by humans to make calculations. Over the centuries, different cultures came up with their own calculating machines. Inca **quipu** threads used knots and the Chinese **suanpan** used counters to keep a tally. During the

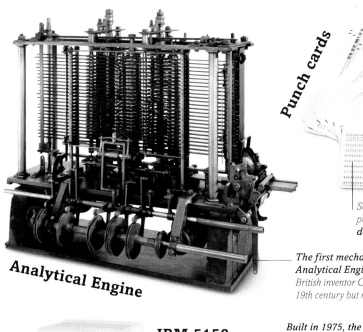

Analytical Engine

Punch cards

Some early computing devices were programmed by punch cards, **which stored data as a pattern of punched holes.**

The first mechanical computer, the **Analytical Engine**, was designed by British inventor Charles Babbage in the 19th century but never fully completed.

*This breakthrough invention from 1971 is a set of electronic circuits that can process a huge amount of information, **allowing computers to carry out a range of functions, instead of just mathematical calculations.***

Intel 4004 microchip

Computers

IBM 5150 personal computer

Built in 1975, the Cray-1 supercomputer was the world's fastest computer *until 1982, when it was overtaken by the Cray X-MP.*

The first of IBM's commercially successful range of personal computers went on sale **in 1981**, *becoming the global standard in computer design.*

Cray 1

The mastermind behind the World Wide Web was British computer scientist Tim Berners-Lee, **who designed a way to link documents on the internet.**

World Wide Web

The first Apple iPhone launched in 2007, featuring a hi-tech touchscreen and a variety of apps.

Russian robot Sophia features the latest artificial intelligence (AI) to **copy human behavior and facial expressions, and engage in basic conversations like a real person.**

Apple iPhone

Sophia

20th century, giant general-purpose computers such as the **ENIAC** were built to make complex calculations. As their capabilities grew, computers shrank in size, from machines that filled entire rooms to microchips such as the **Intel 4004** that could fit on a fingernail. By the 1980s, designs like the **IBM 5150 personal computer** made it easy and affordable for people to have home computers. Computer networks were introduced by the 1960s, but it wasn't until the **World Wide Web** in 1990 that information became linked in the form of the internet. Today, with devices such as smartphones, we can access information at the touch of a button.

Space exploration

Valentina Tereshkova was the first woman to travel into space, in 1963.

Valentina Tereshkova

In 1958, the US launched its first satellite, which discovered belts of radiation surrounding Earth.

Explorer 1

The Soviet Union was the first nation to launch a satellite into orbit around Earth, in 1957.

Yuri Gagarin was the first person to go into orbit around Earth, in 1961.

Yuri Gagarin

The James Webb Space Telescope can look deeper into space than any other observatory—and can even see the earliest stars and galaxies.

Neil Armstrong (left) and Buzz Aldrin (right) were the first astronauts to walk on the moon, in 1969, while Michael Collins remained in the orbiting spacecraft.

Apollo 11 astronauts

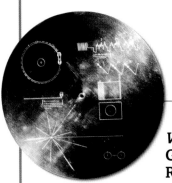

The two Voyager missions each carried a gold-plated record that featured images and sounds from Earth.

Voyager Golden Record

Image taken by the James Webb Space Telescope in 2022

In 1957, the Soviet Union launched the first satellite into space. This was the beginning of the "space race," in which two world superpowers, the Soviet Union and the US, competed to put a person into space. Since then, people have explored the moon and sent probes throughout the solar system.

Following the success of the **Sputnik 1** satellite in 1957, the Soviet Union launched the first man into space, **Yuri Gagarin**, in 1961, followed by the first woman, **Valentina Tereshkova**, two years later. Nevertheless, by 1969, the US had caught up and was able to land **Apollo 11 astronauts** Neil Armstrong and Buzz Aldrin on

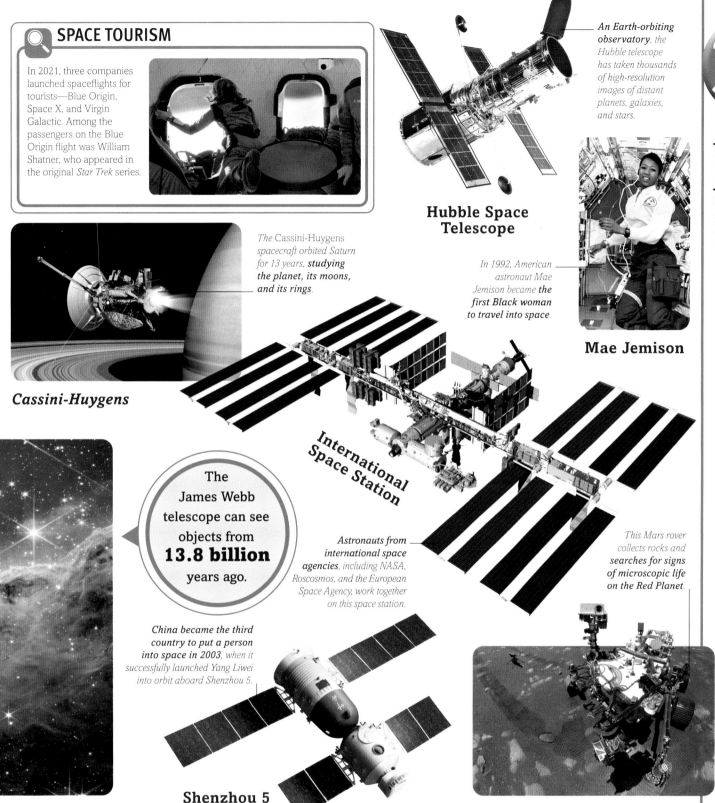

In 2021, three companies launched spaceflights for tourists—Blue Origin, Space X, and Virgin Galactic. Among the passengers on the Blue Origin flight was William Shatner, who appeared in the original *Star Trek* series.

An Earth-orbiting observatory, the Hubble telescope has taken thousands of high-resolution images of distant planets, galaxies, and stars.

Hubble Space Telescope

The Cassini-Huygens *spacecraft orbited Saturn for 13 years, **studying the planet, its moons, and its rings**.*

*In 1992, American astronaut Mae Jemison became **the first Black woman to travel into space**.*

Mae Jemison

Cassini-Huygens

International Space Station

The James Webb telescope can see objects from **13.8 billion** years ago.

*Astronauts from international space **agencies**, including NASA, Roscosmos, and the European Space Agency, work together on this space station.*

*This Mars rover collects rocks and **searches for signs of microscopic life** on the Red Planet.*

***China became the third country to put a person into space in 2003**, when it successfully launched Yang Liwei into orbit aboard Shenzhou 5.*

Shenzhou 5

Perseverance

the moon. Since the 1960s, space probes, such as *Voyager* 1 and 2 and the ***Cassini-Huygens*** spacecraft, have sent back amazing images of the solar system's planets and their moons. The two *Voyager* spacecraft each contain a **Golden Record** with photographs and music from Earth in case they are found by aliens. Other probes, such as ***Perseverance***, have landed on Mars and explored its surface. Scientists have also explored the universe with the help of the **Hubble Space Telescope** and the **James Webb Space Telescope**. These have taken incredible images of some of the oldest stars in the universe.

Modern South America

Chilean president Salvador Allende served for just three years before General Pinochet grabbed power in 1973.

Salvador Allende

Many Indigenous people rely on the Amazon rainforest for their livelihood, and are working to put an end to deforestation in the region.

Amazon deforestation

Tayujin Shuwi Peas and other Indigenous leaders traveled to the US in 2010 to confront the oil company Oxy about the damage it was causing in the Amazon rainforest.

Nobel Peace Prize winner Rigoberta Menchú has spent her life voicing the concerns of Indigenous people, continuing to do so even after her family was killed.

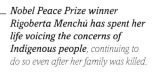

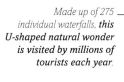

Rigoberta Menchú

Achuar leader Tayujin Shuwi Peas

Made up of 275 individual waterfalls, this U-shaped natural wonder is visited by millions of tourists each year.

Iguazu Falls

South America has changed dramatically in the past 100 years. Citizens across its 12 countries have experienced terrible suffering at times, but brave activists have fought for change. People here are increasingly proud of their continent as it begins to lead the world in several areas.

Chile faced one of its darkest periods when elected president **Salvador Allende** was overthrown by General Pinochet in 1973— a dictator who ruled until 1990. Guatemala witnessed a genocide when the government turned on its Maya community in the 1960s. However, campaigners such as **Rigoberta**

A dramatic dance style that developed in the 19th century in Buenos Aires, the tango is now popular around the world.

Argentine tango

Christ the Redeemer

This 98 ft (30 m) statue of Jesus Christ has watched over Rio de Janeiro in Brazil since 1931.

Lionel Messi

The Indigenous Andean people from across South America are represented by this rainbow-colored flag.

Wiphala flag

One of the earliest South American dances, the cumbia has inspired many others, such as the salsa and merengue.

Messi has won the Ballon d'Or, the FIFA award for the year's best soccer player, seven times.

Paranal Observatory

The world's biggest optical telescope is located at this observatory in Chile's Atacama Desert, where the clear sky makes it easier to observe stars.

Modern South American cities are filled with amazing architecture, such as the Ponte Estaiada bridge in São Paulo, Brazil.

Colombia's national dance, the **cumbia**, was originally a **courtship dance**.

Cumbia

Ponte Estaiada

Menchú kept fighting to stop the violence. More recent voices include Peru's **Achuar leader Tayujin Shuwi Peas**, who stood up against oil pollution in the Amazon River. Despite these difficulties, South America has much to celebrate. Colombia's **cumbia** dance is now popular across South America, while Argentinian soccer player **Lionel Messi** is considered one of the world's best athletes. With countries such as Bolivia honoring their Indigenous people by flying the **Wiphala flag** alongside the national flag, South America is on its way to creating a fully inclusive future.

Postcolonial Africa

Ghanaian flag

A new flag was designed for independent Ghana in which the red stripe signifies struggle, the yellow stands for wealth, and the green represents Ghana's boundless forests.

Colonel Chukwuemeka Ojukwu founded the state of Biafra for Nigeria's Igbo people in 1967, triggering the Nigerian Civil War, in which nearly 2 million people died.

Colonel Ojukwu

Since independence, many African nations have tried to get back their historical artifacts that were stolen by colonial empires, such as this ivory mask, created by the Benin people in the 16th century.

Benin ivory mask

Buganda was a kingdom within Uganda that was abolished after independence, but was reinstated in 1993 under its ruler, Muwenda Mutebi II, the Kabaka.

Fela Kuti was a Nigerian Afrobeat superstar known globally for his songs about colonialism and corruption.

Fela Kuti

Martinican scholar Frantz Fanon was a leading thinker and writer on decolonization who became an ambassador for independent Algeria.

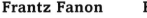

Frantz Fanon

Kabaka of Buganda

There are 54 countries in Africa and most became free of colonial rule in the second half of the 20th century. Over the decades, these nations have faced many challenges, from civil wars to racial discrimination and violence between different ethnic groups. However, in the 21st century, many nations have found greater stability and peace.

In 1957, **Ghana** became the first West African nation to become free of European rule. As more countries gained freedom, there was hope that these new nations would work together to develop—growing their economies, increasing **urbanization**, and sharing cultures. However, many countries had issues of their own to deal with in the immediate aftermath of independence.

Nelson Mandela was an anti-apartheid activist who later became the first Black president of South Africa.

Nelson Mandela

South African Flag

The six-color South African flag has a Y-shaped design, which symbolizes a common path forward for all the nation's citizens.

Major postcolonial African cities have grown at a fast rate, such as Nairobi in Kenya which is now home to more than 4 million people.

Angélique Kidjo is a Grammy Award–winning Beninese singer who is known for her work in campaigning for girls' education, children's rights, and climate change.

African Union

Urbanization

The African Union was created in 2002 to nurture bonds of solidarity and cooperation between African nations.

Angélique Kidjo

Chimamanda Ngozi Adichie is a widely read Nigerian author who has written books about life in postcolonial Nigeria and the legacy of the Nigerian Civil War.

Chimamanda Ngozi Adichie

In Nigeria, ethnic and regional inequalities created by the British Empire caused the Igbo people, led by **Colonel Ojukwu**, to break away, sparking a civil war in 1967. Some countries kept in place colonial laws that were intended to work against the colonized people. For South Africa, the colonial laws of apartheid—where only white people had civil rights—remained in place until 1994, when a new constitution was introduced by President **Nelson Mandela**. Today, many Africans, such as Beninese singer **Angélique Kidjo** and Nigerian writer **Chimamanda Ngozi Adichie**, are vocal about the opportunities and challenges they face.

Skyscrapers

Originally 138 ft (42 m) tall, the building's height was increased to 180 ft (55 m) in 1891.

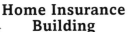

Home Insurance Building

The Empire State Building was the tallest skyscraper in the world for 40 years, until it was surpassed by the World Trade Center in 1971.

The first building in the world to cross the 0.3 mile (0.5 km) mark, Taipei 101 in Taiwan is 1,667 ft (508 m) tall.

The Burj Khalifa has the world's highest **outdoor observation deck**.

Empire State Building

Taipei 101

*The Malaysian Petronas Towers, each 1,483 ft (452 m) tall, are the **world's tallest twin towers**.*

The tallest building in Australia, the Q1 (Queensland Number One) Tower is 1,056 ft (322 m) tall.

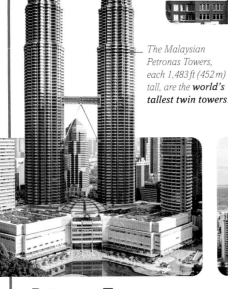

Measuring 2,723 ft (830 m) to the tip, the Burj Khalifa in the UAE is the world's tallest building.

Petronas Towers

Q1 Tower

Burj Khalifa

In the late 19th and early 20th centuries, US architects began to prioritize the use of glass, concrete, and steel in their work. Eventually, this trend spread across the world, and resulted in architects designing buildings so tall that they came to be known as skyscrapers.

It is widely agreed that the **Home Insurance Building**, built in 1885 in Chicago, Illinois, was the world's first skyscraper. Architect William LeBaron Jenney designed it after discovering that thin pieces of steel were strong

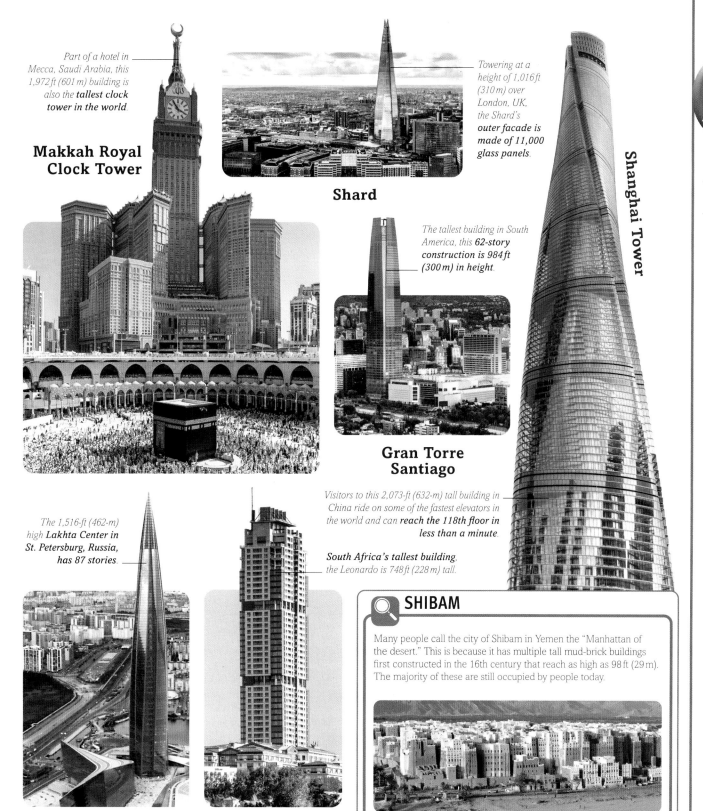

Part of a hotel in Mecca, Saudi Arabia, this 1,972 ft (601 m) building is also the **tallest clock tower in the world**.

Makkah Royal Clock Tower

Towering at a height of 1,016 ft (310 m) over London, UK, the Shard's **outer facade is made of 11,000 glass panels**.

Shard

The tallest building in South America, this **62-story construction is 984 ft (300 m) in height**.

Gran Torre Santiago

Shanghai Tower

The 1,516-ft (462-m) high **Lakhta Center in St. Petersburg, Russia, has 87 stories**.

Visitors to this 2,073-ft (632-m) tall building in China ride on some of the fastest elevators in the world and can **reach the 118th floor in less than a minute**.

South Africa's tallest building, the Leonardo is 748 ft (228 m) tall.

SHIBAM

Many people call the city of Shibam in Yemen the "Manhattan of the desert." This is because it has multiple tall mud-brick buildings first constructed in the 16th century that reach as high as 98 ft (29 m). The majority of these are still occupied by people today.

Lakhta Center   **Leonardo**

enough to support tall buildings. By the early 20th century, there was fierce competition between architects over who could design the tallest building. In 1931, the **Empire State Building** in New York took the crown, reaching a height of 1,453 ft (443 m) up to the tip of its spire. Although the first skyscraper housed a business, subsequent skyscrapers have had different purposes. Many skyscrapers, such as the Australian **Q1 Tower** and the South African **Leonardo**, serve as apartment buildings with thousands of residents. Currently, the world's tallest building is Dubai's **Burj Khalifa**. Constructed in 2009, it has office suites and high-end apartments, as well as luxury hotels.

The digital age

Launched in two bright colors, Apple's 1999 laptop was the first that could connect to the internet wirelessly.

iBook

The BlackBerry, released in 2002, was the first handheld device that could be used to access emails, allowing people to work on the go.

BlackBerry

iPod

Released in 2001, the iPod could hold thousands of digitized songs, and was much lighter than carrying CDs around in a bag.

In a world first, images could be edited and even deleted entirely as soon as they were taken with the D1.

Nikon D1

The Echo works with an inbuilt **digital assistant** called Alexa.

Amazon Echo

*This device has many capabilities, from allowing you to **control lights and other electronics around the home with your voice** to providing reminders for daily tasks.*

Onkyo's wireless, Bluetooth design was the first to allow listeners to roam device-free while taking calls or listening to music.

Bluetooth headphones

Fitbit

*Devices such as the Fitbit can **track** daily physical activity, quality of sleep, and heart rate.*

Modern technology has transformed our daily lives—from how we communicate to how cars work. The digital age has introduced a range of must-have gadgets that have made life easier, while also providing information or help at the touch of a button.

Portable devices, such as the **BlackBerry**, **iBook**, and **iPod**, changed how people communicate, work, and entertain themselves. With the development of digital cameras, such as the **Nikon D1**, people could take thousands of photos and see them instantly, instead of having to print them out. **GPS** technology in cars has replaced oversize

GPS

GPS (Global Positioning Systems) technology uses signals from satellites to pinpoint exact locations, which can assist emergency services during search-and-rescue situations.

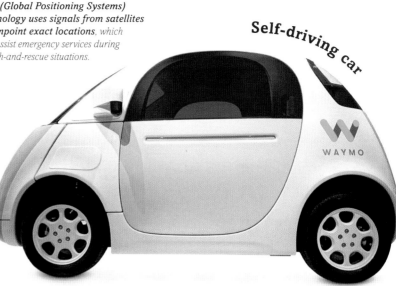

Self-driving car

*Car manufacturing companies have been testing automated cars that can **move by sensing their environment and need no human input**.*

Drone

*Drones can perform many tasks such as **taking aerial photographs, delivering food, and exploring areas humans cannot reach**.*

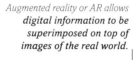

🔍 SOCIAL MEDIA

Staying in touch with people near and far has become easier than it ever was before. Social media platforms allow people to share pictures, try new trends, and watch videos. However, the internet can be a dishonest and unsafe place at times, making it crucial to learn the smartest ways to use it.

*Online meetings allow people from around the world to **work and collaborate with one another remotely**.*

*Augmented reality or AR allows **digital information to be superimposed on top of images of the real world**.*

Augmented reality

Online meetings

maps, making travel easier, and **self-driving cars** can now navigate traffic on their own. During the COVID-19 pandemic, when many people were confined in their houses, the internet helped them stay in touch with their families and allowed work and businesses to function via **online meetings**.

A greener world

*A 19th-century US naturalist, Thoreau immersed himself in the study of nature and is **regarded as the first environmentalist**.*

Henry David Thoreau

*British anthropologist Jane Goodall has worked with apes in Tanzania and is an **activist for wildlife conservation**.*

Jane Goodall

Yellowstone National Park

Greta Thunberg

*Cycle lanes, such as this one in Beijing, China, are designed to keep cyclists safe on the roads and **encourage the use of vehicles that do not harm the environment**.*

Cycle lanes

Wangarī Maathai

*Kenyan environmentalist Wangarī Maathai **founded the Green Belt Movement in 1977, which has now planted more than 50 million trees in her country**.*

*As a young teenager, Swedish climate activist Greta Thunberg **went on a "school strike" to protest against climate change**.*

In the 21st century, planet Earth faces unprecedented problems. Rising pollution levels, climate change, and habitat loss have had devastating effects around the world. But humanity's growing awareness of these issues is the first step toward protecting the planet and creating a brighter future.

Over the past two centuries, factories have produced rising levels of pollution, and spreading cities have taken over forests. Burning fossil fuels (such as coal, oil, and natural gas) to generate energy has added harmful gases to Earth's atmosphere, warming up the planet and changing its climate. Alternative sources of

Established in 1872, Yellowstone National Park was the first of 63 national parks across the US.

*During the 1970s, women from rural India started a conservation movement by **hugging trees to peacefully protect local forests from government plans for logging.***

Chipko Movement

The American bald eagle was on the brink of extinction in 1978, but conservation efforts have resulted in thousands more living in the wild today.

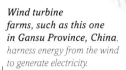
American bald eagle

Wind turbine farms, such as this one in Gansu Province, China, harness energy from the wind to generate electricity.

Wind farm

Plastic pollution in the oceans harms sea creatures, who can swallow it and become ill or die.

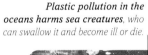

Plastic waste

Indigenous Brazilian activist Txai Suruí was raised in the Amazon rainforest and works to reverse the harmful impact of climate change on her home.

Solar panels

Many buildings today feature solar panels on roofs to absorb sunlight and generate electricity.

OZONE HOLE

High in Earth's atmosphere is a protective layer of ozone gas that absorbs dangerous ultraviolet (UV) radiation from the sun. The use of chemical aerosol sprays releases gases that destroy parts of the ozone layer, leaving holes that allow harmful solar radiation, which can cause diseases such as skin cancer, to reach Earth.

In 2016, scientists conducted a study that proved that the hole in the ozone layer (shown here) is repairing itself due to human efforts.

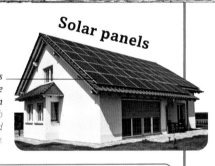
Antarctic ozone hole

Txai Suruí

energy are now being used to harness the power of nature. **Wind farms** and **solar panels** use the wind and sun to generate electricity with minimal pollution. Global efforts to stop deforestation include the **Chipko Movement** in India; the Green Belt Movement by **Wangarĩ Maathai** in Kenya; and the introduction of protected national parks, such as **Yellowstone National Park** in the US. Young environmentalists, including **Greta Thunberg** and **Txai Suruí**, are leading the way by inspiring new generations to take up the cause.

Glossary

Abolitionist
A person who was opposed to the transatlantic slave trade and slavery.

Allies
People or countries working together. In World War I and World War II, the Allies were the countries fighting Germany and other forces.

Alphabet
A group of letters of a language—or group of languages—arranged in a fixed order.

Anti-Semitism
Prejudice and hostility toward Jewish people.

Artillery
Large guns, such as cannons and mortars, or the military units that operate them.

Caliph
The title of a political and religious leader of a caliphate (an Islamic empire).

Capitalism
An economic system based on private ownership of property and competitive conditions for business.

Cavalry
A part of an army made up of troops mounted on horseback.

City-state
A city, and its surrounding territory, that has its own independent government.

Civil rights
The rights of citizens to be socially and politically equal. Black people and other ethnic groups have campaigned to gain the same civil rights as white people, and women have campaigned for the same civil rights as men.

Civil service
All the government departments and employees of a country or state, not including the armed forces.

Civil war
A war between opposing groups of people in the same country.

Civilization
The culture and way of life of people living together in a complex society.

Colonization
The act of sending settlers to establish a colony in another country, often involving taking political control over the people already living there.

Colony
An area under the political control of a foreign state or country.

Communism
An economic system in which ownership of property and wealth is shared.

Constitution
A set of laws that determines the political principles of a government.

Culture
The customs, beliefs, and behavior shared by a society.

Daimyo
A landowning lord in medieval Japan who owed allegiance to the shogun.

Decolonization
The process through which a colonized country gains its political independence from the country or empire that had colonized it.

Dictator
A leader who rules a country alone, with no restrictions on the extent of their power.

Dynasty
A royal family ruling a region, empire, or country for successive generations.

Economy
The system through which goods and services are produced, sold, and bought in a country or region.

Empire
A group of lands or peoples brought under the rule of one government or person.

Epidemic
An outbreak of a contagious disease that spreads rapidly in an area.

Extinct
Describing a species that has completely died out.

Fascism
A political movement stressing nationalism, which places the strength of the state above individual citizens' welfare.

Feudal system
A social system that developed in medieval Europe and Japan, in which lords granted land to people of lower rank in return for loyalty, military assistance, and services.

Genocide
The deliberate killing of a large group of people, especially a whole religious group, race, or nation.

Ghetto
An area of a city where a particular group of people are forced to live, separating them from other inhabitants of the city.

Golden age
A period of great success or development.

Guerrilla warfare
A type of warfare in which small groups of fighters, who are not part of regular uniformed armies, make use of sabotage and surprise attacks against a larger force.

Hominin
A member of the biological group that includes humans and their extinct relatives.

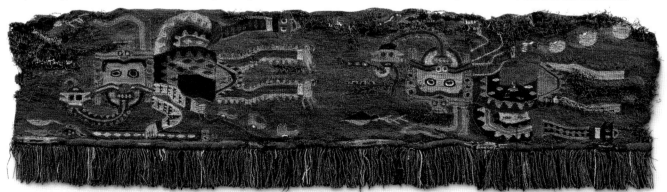

Ice Age

A period when global temperatures drop drastically and large areas of the world are covered by vast sheets of ice. There have been at least five ice ages in Earth's history.

Indigenous

When applied to people, it describes the first or original settlers of a land or region.

Infantry

A part of an army made up of soldiers fighting on foot.

Lacquer

A hard coating added to an object to protect it and provide decoration.

Mausoleum

A large tomb, or an impressive building for housing several tombs.

Medieval period

Also known as the Middle Ages in Europe, the period of history that lasted from about the 5th to the late 15th centuries CE.

Mesopotamia

The region of modern-day Iraq lying close to the Tigris and Euphrates rivers, where many of the earliest civilizations began.

Metalworking

The process of creating or shaping things out of metal.

Monarchy

A type of government in which a king or queen is recognized as the head of state, whether or not they hold real power.

Mosaic

A decoration made from small pieces of glass, stone, or tile, cemented into position to make a picture or pattern.

Mummy

A dead body that has been preserved from decay, either naturally or by artificial means.

Nation

An independent country, or a group of people who share historical or cultural ties.

Nationalism

Loyalty and devotion to a nation, and the political belief that its interests should be pursued as the primary goal of a government.

Neolithic

The period in prehistory when people used complex stone tools, built stone houses, and began to produce pottery.

Nomadic

Describing people who move from place to place without establishing permanent settlements.

Pandemic

An outbreak of a contagious disease that affects the populations of multiple countries around the world.

Peasant

A poor person with few rights who works on the land.

Persecute

To oppress or harass a person or group because of their origins or beliefs.

Philosophy

The study of knowledge and thought. Also, a set of ideas or beliefs.

Plantation

A large farm or estate where the workforce lives on site. Plantations were once common in the Americas and were worked by enslaved people.

Republic

A country that is led by an elected head of state, instead of a monarch or an emperor.

Revolt

An organized uprising intended to overthrow whoever is in authority.

Revolution

A sudden and fundamental change in society brought about by an organized group of protesters. It can also be used to mean a major change in the way that people do or think about things.

Samurai

A Japanese warrior who owed allegiance to a daimyo (a landowning noble) and followed a strict code of honor.

Script

The written characters that make up a writing system, such as an alphabet.

Shogun

A title given to military leaders who ruled Japan in the name of the emperor from the 12th to the 19th centuries.

Siege

A military operation to surround a city or fortress with the intention of capturing it.

Silk Road, The

A system of ancient trade routes from China to West Asia and Europe, named after the most valuable product traded along the routes—silk.

Slavery

The system of treating people as property. Enslaved people have no rights and are not paid for their work.

Soviet Union (USSR)

The Union of Soviet Socialist Republics, a Russian-led communist group of countries that fought on the Allied side in World War II.

Species

A group of organisms that are similar to, and can breed with, each other.

State

A country—or a region within a country—and its people. A state is ruled by a government.

Stele

An upright stone monument, often carved with an inscription. Stelae are set up by rulers to honor the gods, list laws, or mark tombs.

Suffrage

The right to vote in an election. Universal suffrage refers to the right of citizens to vote regardless of their gender, race, wealth, or other factors. Women's suffrage is the right of women to vote on the same basis as men.

Suffragette

Activists who fought for women's right to vote through organized, sometimes, violent protests.

Terra-cotta

A reddish-brown clay that is used for making pottery, sculptures, or ornaments.

Treaty

An official, written agreement between warring parties to bring hostilities to an end.

Urbanization

The large-scale movement of people from rural areas to urban areas such as towns and cities.

Index

ACKNOWLEDGMENTS

Dorling Kindersley would like to thank the following people for their help with making the book: Tom Booth, Agnibesh Das, and Shambhavi Thatte for editorial assistance; Anastasia Baliyan for design assistance; Vagisha Pushp and Manpreet Kaur for picture research assistance; Corey Soper, Dr. Scott Hancock, Professor Nemata Blyden, Dr. Gabriela Ramos, Dr. Leon Rocha, Faith Wilson, Dr. Leanne Holt, and Timothy K. Topper for authenticity checks; Saloni Singh for the jacket; Victoria Pyke for proofreading; and Helen Peters for the index.

Smithsonian Enterprises:
Kealy Gordon, Product Development Manager
Jill Corcoran, Director, Licensed Publishing
Brigid Ferraro, Vice President, Business Development and Licensing
Carol LeBlanc, President

Special thanks to Paige Towler

The publisher would like to thank the following for their kind permission to reproduce their photographs:

(Key: a-above; b-below/bottom; c-center; f-far; l-left; r-right; t-top)

123RF.com: F. Javier Espuny / fxegs 26cl, Mark Green 55tr, maraqu 103crb (ebook), stevanzz 101tl, Ravi weerasinghe 52cla; **africamediaonline.com:** 152-153bc; **akg-images:** 49tl, INTERFOTO / HERMANN HISTORICA GmbH 116ca, Jürgen Sorges 103c; **Alamy Stock Photo:** AB Forces News Collection / U.S. Army photo by Spc. Hubert D. Delany III / 22nd Mobile Public Affairs Detachment 160tl, agefotostock / Christian Goupi 11tr, 119tr, agefotostock / Egmont Strigl 62tr, Agefotostock / Hans-Joachim Schneider 39crb, agefotostock / Historical Views 105tr, 107tc, 130cl, 172cla, agefotostock / Juan García Aunión 17c, agefotostock / Tolo Balaguer 13l, 186tr, Album 102-103cb, 108tr, 116tc, 129tl, Album / British Library 82clb, Stig Alenäs 66ca, Alpha Historica 119tc, 172cb, Alto Vintage Images 141crb, American Photo Archive 155c, Ancient Art and Architecture 23crb, Jules Annan 159cla, Antiqua Print Gallery 135crb, Archivio World 4 18c, Prisma Archivo 2cr, 10cb, 23cb, 66cra, 88cla, 106tr, 139br, Art Collection 77tr, 101tc, 107cr, 138tr, Art Collection 2 110cr, Art Collection 3 87ca, 105bl, Art Directors & TRIP / Helene Rogers 43tl, Arterra Picture Library / Clement Philippe 109tc, Arterra Picture Library / van der Meer Marica 57r, Artokoloro 11cr, 17crb, 40clb, 54-55cb, 66c, 80cl, 112cla, 113ca, 186b, Ashmolean Museum of Art and Archaeology / Heritage Images 33c, Auk Archive 119cr, Sergio Azenha 106cra, Zoltan Bagosi 54cl, Balfore Archive Images 172clb, Ivan Batinic 73cra, Tom Bean 63clb, BG / OLOU 135crb (Eugénie), Zev rad / bibleland 9tc, BibleLandPictures / Zev Radovan 46tr, Zev Radovan / BibleLandPictures 28cra, 30clb, Stuart Black 146bl, Jeffrey Blackler 183tr, Met / Bot 22cla, 49tr, Roland Bouvier 106ca, Pablo Caridad 177cr, Jui-Chi Chan 54cb, CharlineX China Collection 151cla, hencong chen 181tr, Robert K. Chin 152bl, Felix Choo 132cla, Christine Osborne Pictures 73crb, Chronicle 121ca, 134ca, 158tc, cineclassico 111c, Classic Image 129bc, Classic Picture Library 154cra, ClassicStock / SIPLEY 130ca, Clearview 50crb, Christophe Coat 128c, Sorin Colac 90-91, CPA Media Pte Ltd 35tr, 70cla, 96cla, 96c, 97cra (painting), 114cr, 115cr, 176cla, CPA Media Pte Ltd / Pictures From History 28clb, 68crb, 72bc, 78bl, 78bc, 79tl, 82tr, 82-83t, 83cla, 84tr, 84c, 85cr, 85br, 107cla, 113clb, 166cla, CPA Media Pte Ltd / Pictures From History / Victoria and Albert Museum 138-139bc, Ian Dagnall 2tl, 12cr, Danvis Collection 78tl, Darling Archive 69crb, Dasvedanya Archive and News 169cb (seal), David Davis Photoproductions RF 31r, E.R. Degginger 11tc, Danita Delimont / Martin Zwick 67cl, Dinodia Photos RF 53ca, Dinodia Photos RM 139tl, DOD Photo 161br, Douglas Peebles Photography 86cla, 86cl, dpa picture alliance 184l, ephotocorp / Dr. Suresh Vasant 52ca, ephotocorp / Shreekant Jadhav 53tr, Everett Collection Historical 115cb, 153ftl, 155tc, 166ca, 178crb, Everett Collection Inc 143cla, 155cb, 159tr, 173cra, 174ca (Yuri), Peter van Evert 139cr, eye35 126cl, John Vlahidis / EyeEm 160cl, Fine Art

Images / Heritage Images 46clb, funkyfood London - Paul Williams 17cr, 20-21, 68clb, 92-93, Jordi Clave Garsot 147ca, Geopix 175tc, GL Archive 95cr, 116tl, 134cla, 143cra, Glasshouse Images 154cla, Jim Goldstein 177cla, Paul Christian Gordon 63tl, Jeremy Graham 177cla, Granger - Historical Picture Archive 3cl, 40-41c, 43tr, 54cla, 70-71cra, 80bc, 82cla, 96crb, 104tl, 107tr, 116bc, 122-123, 125b, 127tl, 129cra, 130clb, 130-131c, 132-133cb, 133cla, 139tc, 151ca, 154ca, 168ca, 171tl, 171cra, The Granger Collection 97c, 108ca, 127cr, 131tr, Rapp Halour 68tr, 134cl, Shim Harno 72cla, Have Camera Will Travel | Europe 172cra, Hemis 14-15, Hemis.fr / Rieger Bertrand 81cla/1, Heritage Image Partnership Ltd 23cl, 102-103c, 114cla, 118tr, Heritage Image Partnership Ltd / Werner Forman Archive / Canadian Museum of Civilization 63cr, Heritage Image Partnership Ltd / Werner Forman Archive / Churchill Museum 62tl, Heritage Image Partnership Ltd / Werner Forman Archive / National Commission for Museums and Monuments, Lagos 73tl, DAVID HERRAEZ 80cr, Hi-Story 108ca, 127c, Historic Collection 76ca, 153br, History and Art Collection 115tr, The History Collection 70tr, 71clb, 138c, Angelo Hornak 22c, Peter Horree 29cla, 32cra, 34crb, 40ca, 40cb, 50tr, 51l, 88-89, Hum Images 142clb, D. Hurst 130cra, IanDagnall Computing 38cl, 129clb, 150tr, imageBROKER / Martin Siepmann 104tr, imageBROKER / Olaf Schubert 39c, Images & Stories 17t, incamerastock / ICP 58-59, 101cb, 141cb, Interfoto 35cla, 43cl, 43c, 46c, 98-99, 105c, 182-183c, INTERFOTO / Fine Arts 51tc, INTERFOTO / History 125cla, 173cl, INTERFOTO / Personalities 28c, 127c, 140cra, INTERFOTO / Travel 57clb, Ivy Close Images 32ca, 38c, J Marshall - Tribaleye Images 41tr, Japhotos 65clb, John Warburton-Lee Photography / Nigel Pavitt 73cr, Jon Arnold Images Ltd 13crb, Suzuki Kaku 16c, Panagiotis Karapanagiotis 30bc, Robert Kawka 38cla, 39clb, Georgios Kollidas 39bl, Terese Loeb Kreuzer 28cla, Elitsa Lambova 40cl, Lebrecht Music & Arts 102clb, Lebrecht Music & Arts / Lebrecht 149tr, Bruce Leighty 132c, frans lemmens 105tl, LMA / AW 34l, Loop Images Ltd / Jan Holm 18bc, Barney Low 160cr, Magite Historic 67bl, Markus Mainka 180crb, mambo 32-33cb, Hilke Maunder 60-61b, mauritius images GmbH / Hans Blossey 105br, Antony McAulay 182br, Mcphoto / Otf / Blickwinkel 10cla, Hercules Milas 23clb, 66br, Trinity Mirror / Mirrorpix 178cra, Alexander Mitrofanov 151cra, Jeff Morgan 02 179br, Dmitriy Moroz 28cr, Museum of London / Heritage-Images 153ca, The Museum of East Asian Art / Heritage Images 45cb, Natural History Museum, London 12ca, Newscom 76-77c, NG Images 175cra, Niday Picture Library 69cra, 78-79bc, 141tr, North Wind Picture Archives 51tl, 101crb, 108clb, 118c, 118-119c, 131crb, Walter Oleksy 138cl, Jonathan ORourke 60clb, 87tl, PAINTING 100c, Viktor Pazemin 147b, Peregrine 106cb, Peter Adams Photography 184-185tc, Photo 12 65tl, Photononstop / Philippe Turpin 183br, PhotoStock-Israel / Historic Illustrations 120clb, Pictorial Press Ltd 134tr, 135tl, 135tr, 149tl, 151cb, 184cla, Pictorial Press Ltd / Roscosmos 174tr, picture 141c, The Picture Art Collection 67tr, 83c, 104bl, 134clb, PictureLux / The Hollywood Archive 150bl, Juan Diego Oliva Plaza 182bl, PR Archive 132clb, Premier 32cla, The Print Collector 136-137, The Print Collector / CM Dixon / Heritage Images 12crb, 44cla, The Print Collector / Heritage Images 78cr, 174cl, 187clb, Pump Park Vintage Photography 114crb, Kent Raney 61tl, Really Easy Star 30-31c, Really Easy Star / Toni Spagone 53tl, Robert Harding World Imagery 39cb, Robertharding 5bl, 23cla, 54tr, Robertharding / Adam Woolfitt 42tl, Royal Armouries Museum 81cla, Maurice Savage 168cla, Science History Images 49cr, 64ca, 65tr, 71br, 83cra, 104cl, 155tl, 168cb, 172tr, 172-173cb, 180tl, Science History Images / Photo Researchers 79c, 101cra, 133ca, 140cla, 173tc, Science Museum, London, UK / Lebrecht Music & Arts / Derek Bayes 106cla, Science Photo Library 177cr, Christopher Scott 74-75, William Scott 13ca, Shawshots 157r, Süddeutsche Zeitung Photo 148tr, Süddeutsche Zeitung Photo / Stefan Klein 163br, Sueddeutsche Zeitung Photo / Scherl 139tr, SuperStock / Cosmo Condina 126-127cb, Keith Taylor 41crb, The Canadian Press / Graeme Roy 182c, The Print Collector / CM Dixon 42-43cb, 47tr, ThePhotoMender.com 133cra, Alison Thompson 106clb, Andrew Twort 169cb, United Archives GmbH / IFTN 159crb, UtCon Collection 168tr, Greg Vaughn 108cl, Ivan Vdovin 47c, 80c, 97crb, Vkstudio 35clb, Watchtheworld 73tr, Ken Welsh 16ca, Werner Forman Archive / British Museum, London / Heritage Images 13cr, Werner Forman Archive / E.

Acknowledgments

Strouhal / Heritage Images 24-25, Werner Forman Archive / National Museum, Copenhagen / Heritage Images 42tc, Edward Westmacott 67cr, WILDLIFE GmbH 57cb, Chris Willson 182tr, World Discovery 79cl, World History Archive 5br, 38cra, 46crb, 57tl, 102cra, 103tl, 126clb, 167cr, 174clb, Xinhua / Zhang Yuwei 153tr, Akihito Yokoyama 104cb, ZUMA Press, Inc. 167cra, 176cra, ZUMA Press, Inc. / SIPA Asia 38tl; **Shreya Anand:** 103crb; **Anandajoti Bhikkhu:** 30ca; **Ardea:** Paulo Di Oliviera 185c; **Maxime Aubert, Griffith University:** 13tr; **Bridgeman Images:** 28cb, 56-57c, 68tl, 69tl, 69tc, 100cla, 108-109c, Archives Charmet 26cra, Dirk Bakker 3clb, 54ca, 63cl, Derek Bayes 87cl, © Boltin Picture Library 23clb (Muisca), Boltin Picture Library 88clb, Bonhams, London, UK 35crb (Pendant), British Library Board. All Rights Reserved 41clb, CERN / Novapix 173cr, © Archives Charmet 70ca, Christie's Images 103tc, Andrea Jemolo 81cl, Photo Josse 100cb, 103cra, 127cb, King, Marcus (20th century) / New Zealander 125tr, Museum of Fine Arts, Houston / Museum purchase funded by the Agnes Cullen Arnold Endowment Fund and the McAshan Educational and Charitable Trust 31ca, Museum of London 153tl, National Army Museum 112cra, NPL - DeA Picture Library 126cla, Peter Newark American Pictures 131cr, Peter Newark Military Pictures 109crb, Photo © Photo Josse 69tl (coin), Pictures from History 41tl, PVDE 184ca, Zev Radovan 29cl, Heini Schneebeli 57c, 72ca, Smithsonian Institution 128cr, Spaarnestad Photo 140ca, Tarker 139ca, The Israel Museum / Meidad Suchowolski 18-19tc, Don Troiani. All Rights Reserved 2022 5cr, 131tl, 131ca, Werner Forman Archive 31c; **© The Trustees of the British Museum. All rights reserved:** 19tr, 43br, 45tl, 57tc, 61cr, 120tc; **Collection of the Smithsonian National Museum of African American History and Culture:** 118bc, 170cra, Gift of Oprah Winfrey 119ftr; **Dorling Kindersley:** Rob Reichenfeld / Bishop's Museum, Hawaii 87tr, Board of Trustees of the Royal Armouries / Gary Ombler 81tl, 129bl, 132t, Alistair Duncan / Cairo Museum 33tr, Combined Military Services Museum (CMSM) / Gary Ombler 81tr, Andy Crawford 3cr, / Trustees of the National Museums Of Scotland 65cr, 175tc (telescope), Dave King / Durham University Oriental Museum 77ca, Durham University Oriental Museum / Gary Ombler 38tc, Gary Ombler / Durham University Oriental Museum 113tr, Steve Gorton / Eden Camp Museum 2cb, Gary Ombler / the Ermine Street Guard 31cl, Simon Mumford / The Flag Institute 179tr, Dave King / Gettysburg National Military Park 141cla, J. Kershaw / © The Trustees of the British Museum. All rights reserved 53cr, James Mann / Colin Laybourn / P&A Wood 143crb, Gary Ombler / National Cycle Collection 142cr, Gary Ombler / © The Board of Trustees of the Armouries 70clb, Gary Ombler / Adrian Shooter 142-143cb, Gary Ombler / R. Florio 143cr, Order of the Black Prince / Geoff Dann 81crb, Graham Rae 3b, / Hellenic Maritime Museum 31tc, Dave Rudkin / RAF Museum, Hendon 169cl, Gary Ombler / Railroad Museum of Pennsylvania 127crb, Royal Armouries, Leeds / Gary Ombler 81t, Gary Ombler / Scale Model World, Rick Williams 146cr, Clive Streeter / The Science Museum, London 155cra, Dave King / The Science Museum 126ca, Mike Dunning / Science Museum, London 127tc, Gary Ombler / Shuttleworth Collection 143tr, Martin Cameron / Shuttleworth Collection, Bedfordshire 143tl, Gary Ombler / University of Aberdeen 27ca, 28cl, Gary Ombler / University of Pennsylvania Museum of Archaeology and Anthropology 28ca, 29r, 30cla, 102cla, Tina Chambers and James Stevenson / University Museum of Newcastle 31clb, 31clb (sword), University of Aberdeen / Gary Ombler 117ca, Vikings of Middle England / Gary Ombler 67c, 81cra/1, Geoff Dann / Wallace Collection, London 113tl, Gary Ombler / Wardrobe Museum, Salisbury 158tl, Gary Ombler / Whipple Museum of History of Science, Cambridge 106cr; **Dreamstime.com:** Yuriy Afonkin 108cla/1, Anton Aleksenko 32c, Alenmax 150cl, Alessandro0770 65c, Angellodeco 50cla, Antonella865 95tl, Rui Baião 78tc, Robert Paul Van Beets 158cb, Beibaoke1 70crb, Roman Belogorodov 182tl, Philip Bird 142cl, Oleg Blazhyievskyi 85ca, Florian Blümm 35cra, Maurice Brand 56clb, Coatchristophe 26-27b, Cowardlion 35c, Kobby Dagan 111br, Nicolas De Corte 118cla, Chris Dorney 169clb, Chanchai Duangdoosan 76cr, Dudlajzov 17cl, Espiegle 176cb, F11photo 177crb, Alexandre Fagundes De Fagundes 96ca, Santiago Rodríguez Fontoba 30crb, Frenta 114c, Guppyimages 178cla, Anastasiia Guseva 179clb, Hupeng 2br, 143cl, Praveen Indramohan 80-81bc, Isselee 16clb, Jackmalipan 162clb, Attila Jandi 47cr, Javarman 181crb, Kanokphoto 57cl, Chris Kelleher 109cra, Ferenc Kósa 135ca, Anna Krivitskaia 62bc, Mirko Kuzmanovic 33cr, 134cr, Istvan Ladanyi 16cr, Fabio Lamanna 52-53c, Aija Lehtonen 179c, Lightbrush701 17clb, Chun-tso Lin 16tc, Vezhoyi Lohe 162bl, Lalam Mandavkar 35crb, Marchello74 177tc, Sergey Mayorov 28-29t, Vladimir Melnik 65br, Meoita 161tr, Martin Mette 79tc, Mistervlad 3tl, 88bc, Neezhom 163tr, Neophuket 113crb, Nicousnake 85c, Boonlong Noragitt 51c, Alexey Novikov 181clb, Dmitry Orlov 64cla, Osoznaniejizni 18tc, Oxfordsquare 185cr, Marcus Scott-parkin 100bl, Sean Pavone 84-85cb, Pictac 108cla, David Pillow 34cra, Plnirem 16crb, Ian Poole 168c, Radiokafka 34-35c, Rangizzz 108cla/2, Rhombur 50clb, Rixie 42bc, Mauro Rodrigues 48c, Dmitry Rukhlenko 53crb, Jorge Salcedo / Jorgeantonio 124bl, Spectral-design 129ca, Taiga 69tr, Tifonimages 181ca, Tloventures 133tc, Toxawww 173crb, Vladimir Tronin 83tr, Nicoleta Raluca Tudor 42c, Ultraone 51cra, VanderWolfImages 160tr, Sergio Delle Vedove 67tc, Vincentstthomas 77cr, Taras Vyshnya 180clb, Joshua Wanyama 179cr, 187br, Imogen Warren 86tr, Danny Washburn 63tr, Whpics 34fcra, 89tc, Noppasin Wongchum 159cr, Jeff Workman 160cb, King Ho Yim 55c, Alexandr Yurtchenko 86cr, Evgeny Kharitonov 55tl; **ESA:** NASA 144-145; **Kenneth Garrett:** 12cra; **Getty Images:** AFP / Jewel Samad 168r, Daniel Leal / AFP 171crb, Leon Neal / AFP 169tc (Noor), Oli Scarff / AFP 185cl, Timothy A. Clary / AFP 169crb, Agence France Presse 170-171c, The Asahi Shimbun 169tr, Toni Anne Barson / Contributor 176cl, Best View Stock 115l, Bettmann 109c, 130c, 131cra, 150-151bc, 151tr, 151br, 156br, 159cra, 163tl, 164-165, 170ca, 170cb, Bettmann / Contributor 155cl, Bloomberg 181cb, Bloomberg / Doug Kanter 185cra, Gabriel Bouys / Staff 176c, Buyenlarge 156tc, China News Service / Tian Bing 161cra, ClassicStock 119tl, Corbis Historical 166-167cb, Corbis Historical / Adoc-Photos 151tl, Corbis Historical / Fine Art / VCG Wilson 38-39cb, Corbis Historical / Leemage 44tr, Corbis Historical / Micheline Pelletier 184crb, Jean-Pierre Courau 88c, De Agostini / DEA / A. C. Cooper 45tc, De Agostini / DEA / A. Jemolo 30cl, De Agostini / DEA / G. Dagli Orti 8cra, 29ca, 44cl, 44-45t, De Agostini Editorial / Dea / G. Dagli Orti 42tr, Dea / A. Dagli Orti / Contributor 22ca, 22-23tc, DEA / A. Dagli Orti / De Agostini 66cl, DEA / G. Dagli Orti 96clb, 96-97tc, DEA / G. DAGLI ORTI / De Agostini 129tr, DEA / G. DAGLI ORTI / De Agostini Editorial 48cr, DEA / L. DE MASI / De Agostini Editorial 19br, Dea Picture Library / Contributor 76cla, 76cra, DEA Picture Library / De Agostini 44cb, 120crb, DEA Picture Library / De Agostini Editorial 18fclb, 47tl, Deagostini / DEA / A. Dagli Orti 159tl, Werner Forman 62c, 62cr, The Frent Collection / David J. & Janice L. Frent / Corbis 171tc, Alain Mingam / Gamma-Rapho 167tr, Jerome Chatin / Gamma-Rapho 6-7, Sergio Gaudenti 162cla, GraphicaArtis / Archive Photos 166clb, Louise Gubb / Contributor 179cla, Henry Guttmann Collection / Stringer 156tl, Heritage Images 135cl, 152tr, 162tl, Heritage Images / Hulton Archive 170cl, Hulton Archive 158tr, Hulton Archive / Apic 173tr, Hulton Archive / Art Media / Print Collector 32clb, Hulton Archive / Heritage Images / Fine Art Images 72tr, Hulton Archive / Print Collector / CM Dixon 67br, Hulton Fine Art Collection / Art Images 72-73c, The Image Bank Unreleased / Dinodia Photo 113cr, Imagno / brandstaetter images / Hulton Archive 169tc, The India Today Group 185tc, Ken Florey Suffrage Collection / Gado 152-153c, Keystone / Stringer 163cr, Keystone-France / Gamma-Keystone 151ca/1, 158c, LightRocket / John S Lander 116clb, Saverio Marfia 110cra, G. Milne 157tl, Moment / Anand Purohit 81cra, Moment / Ayzenstayn 13tc, Moment / Gary Samples 185tr, Moment / Luis Dafos 121crb, MPI / Stringer 71cr, NurPhoto / Contributor 177tr, PhotoQuest 157cl, PhotosIndia.com 111l, Pictures from History / Contributor 96bc, Pictures From History / Universal Images Group 80tr, 117br, 166cra, Joe Daniel Price 35tl, Print Collector 18bl, 152c, Fred Ramage / Stringer 162ca, Probal Rashid 119br, Science & Society Picture Library 4br, 83cr, 101ca, 126cra, 127ca, 140-141cb, 141cl, 142ca, 173tl, Pascal J Le Segretain / Contributor 178cr, Sepia Times / Contributor 76crb, Leni Sinclair / Contributor 178c, Prakash Singh / AFP / Staff 161tl, Carl Court / Staff 117cl, STF / AFP 166cl, HIGH-G Productions / Stocktrek Images 160cra, Stocktrek Images 175c, Stringer / Dieter Nagl 148tl, Tetra Images 128clb, The Image Bank Unreleased / Chris Hellier 69cr, The Image Bank Unreleased / Richard T. Nowitz 109cla, U.S. Navy / Handout / Kenneth Moll 161bl, Universal History Archive 49tc, 149cr, 154clb, Universal History Archive / Universal Images Group 150cla, 158-159cb, Universal History Archive / UniversalImagesGroup 100-101c, 112r, UniversalImagesGroup / Contributor 23tr, VCG / Contributor 2bl, 22r, Roger Viollet 158clb, Visual China Group / Dong Yiming 184cr, Phil Walter 111cr; **Getty Images / iStock:** agshotime 82cr, Arturbo 48clb, BrasilNut1 97cla, Derek Brumby 162cb, destillat 41cra, E+ / Bartosz Hadyniak 45r, E+ / CT757fan 160cla, E+ / Gargolas 36-37, Eloi_Omella 154bl, Pawel Gaul 50-51ca, holgs 39cr, Vinayak Jagtap 45clb, kirill4mula 64crb, Stephan Kogelman 111tr, mtcurado 118cl, NicolasMcComber 180fclb, ntrifunovic 180ca, R.M. Nunes 85tr, OscarCatt 100ca, Sean Pavone 155crb, 180r, Plainview 110clb, Andrey Popov 183bl, Ridofranz 183cr, Roki Rodic 129cla, Smartstock 128cb, tankbmb 86-87cb, Valdisskudre 181tc, zim286 160crb; **Library of Congress, Washington, D.C.:** 00695813 / Zhang, Yushu, Teishō Tsuga, and Japanese Rare Book Collection. 114tr; **© The Metropolitan Museum of Art:** 3tr, 19cr, 42bl, 47bl, 49cl, 62bl, 63ca, 84cl, 85tl, 85bc, 88ca, 89bc, 104cr, 110cl, 110fcla (mime sculpture), 120cl, 120c, 120-121tc, 120-121bc, 121cr, 128tl, 187tr, Bequest of Benjamin Altman, 1913 97tl, 114clb, Gift of The American Society for the Excavation of Sardis, 1926 23tc, Purchase, Bequest of Dorothy Graham Bennett, 1993 71tl, Bequest of Alice K. Bache, 1977 94cr, Bequest of Jane Costello Goldberg, from the Collection of Arnold I. Goldberg, 1986 3crb, 31cb, Bequest of Joseph H. Durkee, 1898 52cra, 112ca, Bequest of William S. Lieberman, 2005 117tl, Gift of Heber R. Bishop, 1902 115crb, The Cesnola Collection, Purchased by subscription, 1874–76 40c (jug), Edith Perry Chapman Fund, 1975 23cr (Staff), Gift of Charles and Valerie Diker, 1999 54crb, Fletcher Fund, 1937 5bc, 40c, Fletcher Fund, 1940 34c, Mr. and Mrs. Isaac D. Fletcher Collection, Bequest of Isaac D. Fletcher and Rogers Fund, by exchange, 1985 64-65cb, Funds from various donors, 1886 (86.1.14, .18, .21, .28) 33tc, Gift of Bashford Dean, 1914 79cr, Gift of J. Pierpont Morgan, 1917 68-69c, Gift of John M. Crawford Jr., in honor of Professor Wen Fong, 1984 41ca, Gift of Joseph W. Drexel, 1889 100cra, Gift of Lincoln Kirstein, 1959 124cr, Gift of Mrs. V. Everit Macy, 1923 117cb, Gift of Oxford University Expedition to Nubia, 1926 44clb, H. O. Havemeyer Collection, Bequest of Mrs. H. O. Havemeyer, 1929 117cra, Harris Brisbane Dick Fund, 1949 33cl, Gift of Mr. and Mrs. Jack A. Josephson, 1976 65tc, Purchase, Mrs. Richard E. Linburn Gift, 1987 71cb, Gift of Henry G. Marquand, 1882 55cr, Jan Mitchell and Sons Collection, Gift of Jan Mitchell, 1991 1, 23cr, Gift of Norbert Schimmel Trust, 1989 2cra, 22clb, Purchase, 1895 67tl, Purchase, Arthur Ochs Sulzberger Gift, 2002 81crb (Cannon), Purchase, Bequest of Dorothy Graham Bennett, 2006 30tc, Purchase, Florence and Herbert Irving Gift, 1991 53cla, Purchase, Harris Brisbane Dick Fund and The Vincent Astor Foundation Gift, 1984 113tc, Purchase, Joseph Pulitzer Bequest, 1918 117tr, Purchase, Mary and James G. Wallach Foundation Gift, in celebration of the Museum's 150th Anniversary, 2020 78tr, Purchase, Mr. and Mrs. Ronald S. Lauder Gift and Louis V. Bell, Harris Brisbane Dick, Fletcher, and Rogers Funds and Joseph Pulitzer Bequest, 2016 49c, Purchase, The Kurt Berliner Foundation Gift, 2000 67bc, Purchase, The Vincent Astor Foundation Gift, 2010 5tr, 82c, Ralph T. Coe Collection, Gift of Ralph T. Coe Foundation for the Arts, 2011 132cra, The Michael C. Rockefeller Memorial Collection, Bequest of Nelson A. Rockefeller, 1972 178cl, The Michael C. Rockefeller Memorial Collection, Gift of Nelson A. Rockefeller, 1963 54c, Rogers Fund, 1908 44-45ca, Rogers Fund, 1941 65crb, The Michael C. Rockefeller Memorial Collection, Bequest of Nelson A. Rockefeller, 1979 45cla, 54cr, Theodore M. Davis Collection, Bequest of Theodore M. Davis, 1915 33crb, 64tr; **MUVS, Vienna:** 153cr; **NASA:** 174ca, ESA, CSA, and STScI 174-175cb, JPL-Caltech / MSSS 175crb; **NOAA:** 185crb; **Onkyo:** 182cb (Onkyo bluetooth headphones); **Science Photo Library:** Mauricio Anton 12cla, Central Intelligence Agency 169ca, David Ducros 175cla, Library Of Congress 168clb, Raul Martin 10bl, 10-11tc, Tom Mchugh 18clb, Natural History Museum, London 11br, 12tr, David Parker 183c, Detlev Van Ravenswaay 175cb, John Reader 8bl, 10cra, Javier Trueba 10ca; **Shutterstock.com:** 169cr, Anonymous / AP 167ca, 171ca, Khaled Elfiqi / EPA 102cl, Everett Collection 118cra, 154crb, fotohunter 94-95b, Roberto Galan 176-177c, Johnathan21 77crb, Julien'sAuctions / Bournemouth News 167cla, Keitma 9b, KoreaKHW 77c, MattiaATH 163ca, Trong Nguyen 83clb, saiko3p 84ctc, Samareen 181cla, Renata Sedmakova 35clb, sianstock 50ca, Sipa 167crb, smith371 76clb, The LIFE Picture Collection / Mark Kauffman 162-163c, Two discs of turquoise and shell (and possibly jet), portraying alternating stylised representations of a bird and a feline, perhaps a condor and a puma / Werner Forman Archive 44crb; **SuperStock:** A. Burkatovski / Fine Art Images 2tr, 56cb; **TopFoto:** 152cla; **U.S. Air Force:** 149cl; **The University Of Auckland:** Courtesy of the Anthropology Photographic Archive, Department of Anthropology 87c; **Wellcome Collection:** Model of a foot operated drill, Germany, 1910-1920. Science Museum, London. Attribution 4.0 International (CC BY 4.0) 140cr, Early inhaler for ether anaesthesia, London, England, 1847-1. Science Museum, London. Attribution 4.0 International (CC BY 4.0) 141ca, Stethoscope, England, 1834-1840. Science Museum, London. Attribution 4.0 International (CC BY 4.0) 141cra, Science Museum, London 35fcrb; **Wikipedia:** 129br, Fanghong 39tl, Marie-Lan Nguyen / National Museum of Antiquities of Tajikistan 38tr

All other images © Dorling Kindersley
For further information see: **www.dkimages.com**

OUR WORLD IN PICTURES

BOOKS

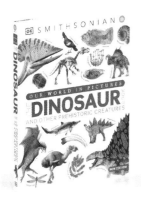

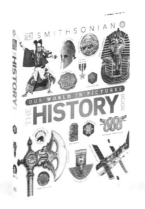
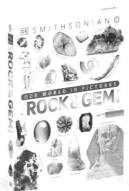

FLASH CARDS

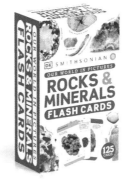

 For the curious